# SOUTHERN INSPIRATION

## 140
## Home Plans Inspired
## by the American South

# SOUTHERN INSPIRATION

*140 Home Plans Inspired by the American South*

79

Published by Hanley Wood
One Thomas Circle, NW, Suite 600
Washington, DC 20005

Distribution Center
29333 Lorie Lane
Wixom, Michigan 48393

Group Publisher, Andrew Schultz
Associate Publisher, Editorial Development, Jennifer Pearce
Managing Editor, Hannah McCann
Senior Editor, Nate Ewell
Associate Editor, Simon Hyoun
Senior Plan Merchandiser, Nicole Phipps
Plan Merchandiser, Hillary Huff
Proofreader/Copywriter, Dyana Weis
Graphic Artist, Joong Min
Plan Data Team Leader, Susan Jasmin
Production Manager, Brenda McClary
Contributing Editor, Elena Marcheso Moreno

Vice President, Retail Sales, Scott Hill
National Sales Manager, Bruce Holmes
Director, Plan Products, Matt Higgins

Most Hanley Wood titles are available at quantity discounts with bulk purchases
for educational, business, or sales promotional use. For information, please contact
Bruce Holmes at bholmes@hanleywood.com.

BIG DESIGNS, INC.
President, Creative Director, Anthony D'Elia
Vice President, Business Manager, Megan D'Elia
Vice President, Design Director, Chris Bonavita
Editorial Director, John Roach
Assistant Editor, Patricia Starkey
Senior Art Director, Stephen Reinfurt
Production Director, David Barbella
Photo Editor, Christine DiVuolo
Graphic Designer, Frank Augugliaro
Graphic Designer, Billy Doremus
Graphic Designer, Jacque Young
Assistant Production Manager, Rich Fuentes

PHOTO CREDITS
Front Cover and Preceding Page: Courtesy of Chadsworth's Columns.
Photographer: Kenneth S. Collier. For details, see page 82.
This Page: Andy Lautman, Lautman Photography.
Facing Page Right: Courtesy of William E. Poole Designs, Inc.
Facing Page Left: Andy Lautman, Lautman Photography.
Back Cover: Mark Englund. For details, see page 22.

10 9 8 7 6 5 4 3 2 1

Printed in the United States of America

Library of Congress Control Number: 2005927713
ISBN-13: 978-1-931131-41-4
ISBN-10: 1-931131-41-4

# Contents

# New Homes from the Old South

**Above: Double story porches, columns, and arched windows give this modern home all the charm of a classic Colonial house of the Old South. Right: A grand entrance is a staple of Southern architecture.**

The allure of the South is hard to resist. It has a captivating charm and timeless beauty characterized by its geography and by its history. From city to countryside, Southern culture is steeped in tradition. The Southern states have their own customs, cuisine, and architecture, and Southern landscapes are dotted with some of the loveliest homes in the nation.

With fertile soil, a warm, mild climate, and a generous balance of sun and rain, Colonial farmers capitalized on the land in the South. From Maryland to Georgia and from the mountains to the ocean, plantations developed, and as they spread the regional architecture emerged, from rough shelters in the beginning, to 17th Century farmhouses, to 18th Century plantations, to 19th Century mansions.

Southern architecture is at the core of gracious living, and the very essence of the region's style. Inspiration for Southern home design takes many forms, but is always welcoming and steeped in tradition. Regardless of style, the Southern home speaks with one voice of the enduring culture and regional influences from a time and place where home and family were important, and when a slower pace meant they could be enjoyed fully.

House architecture of the South has its roots in Europe. Greek Revival, Georgian, Federal, and plantation manor houses were all based on European designs, many brought over from England in pattern books by the carpenters and masons who would eventually build the historic homes. Even the Floridian style, with its Caribbean flair, is influenced by the architecture of the Mediterranean.

The past is still very much respected in the South, and this book includes many traditional-style homes. New home designs often emulate the best features of the historic Colonial styles so loved in the South, but they do not strictly adhere to bygone dictates of interior space. Rather than cramped rooms and chopped up floor plans, the architects and designers whose works are portrayed here create new Southern homes with the open vistas and flowing spaces suitable to contemporary lifestyles. Then they borrow important details and ornament from the past as they establish a new evolution of Southern Inspiration. ■

# Southern Style

# Evolving Farmhouse Style

What is Southern architecture? It is a collection of Colonial designs that emerged over time in the American South. It is also a series of innovative trends that evolved along with the social, economic, and political culture in a young nation searching for its own identity and its own styles.

Farmhouses and plantation homes comprise much of the South's early architecture. Relatively modest at first, plantation homes grew to more elaborate proportions as the wealth of the Southern planters grew. By the Civil War, grand and gracious plantation homes were seen throughout all the Southern states, from Maryland to Florida.

These large estates often boasted a grand manor house, numerous outbuildings, and many slaves. But smaller, family-oriented farms were just as likely to have homes that would inspire generations of farmhouse design.

As the same time plantations were expanding, the popular style of architecture in the Old South was changing from the English-inspired Georgian Colonial styles of the 18th Century to a more American look. Plantation home styles followed the same trend.

Traditional farmhouse floor plans are usually rectangular. In the hot South they might be long and somewhat narrow to catch the breezes. Today, the image of a plantation home is one of a rambling farmhouse, with long low lines and extensive wraparound porches with deep overhangs. Southern farmhouse plans are noted for their distinctive pitched roofs, box-like forms, and simple styling.

**Left: A boxy shape, long, low windows, and a breezy porch easily identify this vernacular Southern farmhouse. Top: Relaxed, large covered porches that wrap around corners are distinct Southern farmhouse details.**

# Southern Style

# The New American Architecture

Architectural styles changed in the late 18th Century to reflect the Colonists' new independence, and a uniquely American-style home emerged, which borrowed from the greatly admired Georgians that were so prevalent in the South.

Federalist homes today are finely crafted. Often clad in brick or clapboard, they are elaborately decorated. Slim columns or pilasters and sidelights at the front door are defining features, and symmetrical windows outlined by shutters, semi-circular fanlights, and arches are common. Old Southern Federalist homes always had multipaned windows because it was difficult to make larger pieces of glass at the time, and this charming detail is still recreated today. The modern Federalist home might include elliptical or Palladian windows and look much like its older counterpart, but could also have symmetrical wings added to the main house to accommodate a garage at one end, and additional living space at the other.

Applied ornament and delicate details both outside and inside are traditional hallmarks of this style, which was greatly influenced by the ancient temples of Greece and Rome. Interiors can be quite formal, with oval-shaped rooms, recessed wall arches, and decorative trim, such as swags and garlands. All these flourishes of the past are included in space that is more open and free-flowing than the smaller rooms of the original Federalist homes.

**Above: Building symmetry, balance, and proportion—along with exterior details like arched windows—are some of the enduring qualities of Federalist-style homes. Left: Rather than strict and limiting imitation, open and inviting modern interior spaces hint at the American Federalist period with arched openings and fanlight windows.**

## Of Time and Place

While the Greek Revival plantation house Tara of *Gone with the Wind* was in fact a stage set, it embodies much of the 21st Century's image of the houses that were built in the Old South. Antebellum manor houses of the style that was popular before the Civil War were the homes of wealthy Southerners and many of them were destroyed in the war between the North and the South. Yet some lovely examples of these homes still remain and they serve as the Southern inspiration for new home designs in many regions.

Rather than a horizontal front facade, a Greek Revival home has a gable end presentation. Hipped roofs and gables are low pitched and the cornice trim is substantial. Full-height classical columns mark a grand entrance and

**Top:** The ornamented columns supporting a front portico and the front entry's gable-end presentation are unmistakably Southern details in this Greek Revival home design. **Left:** Tall ceilings, soaring columns, and statuary are all contemporary design approaches that evoke the Greek Revival manor house of the antebellum South.

prominent balconies often adorn the front and back.

The modern rendidition of a Greek Revival home has the grand interior spaces, curved staircases, and soaring ceilings found in the historic manor houses of the Old South. Gracious, full-height windows are lovely details borrowed successfully from the past. Two-story foyers provide elegant entrances, and the classical columns that support entrances and porticos are often used again inside to outline "rooms" in open interior spaces. While the public spaces are often formal, there is plenty of room in this style for more casual living areas, as well.

**Above: Highly ornamented columns and a sweeping staircase are European touches that would be equally at home in a manor house of the Old South as in a new Southern home of gracious proportions.**

# Southern Style

Above: This contemporary Floridian graciously blends a Mediterranean design with Southern Colonial details like a two-story entry, soaring classical columns, and American Federalist-derived arched entries and delicate ornamentation.
Right: The elegant covered lanai here is an outside living room for all four seasons.

# Fantastic Floridians

Floridian home plans blend Mediterranean design with Southern Colonial architecture to create a truly unique American style. The basic concept of the Floridian home hasn't changed much since it first appeared at the turn of the 20th Century. It still relies on keeping the heat out while letting the light in. Low-pitched roofs, wide eaves, and pastel colors are some of the aesthetically pleasing approaches to managing the sun.

Interiors of these homes are formal but also relaxed, and open floor plans tend to be generously sized. Floridian-style homes are famous for melding indoor rooms and outdoor spaces into a single living area. One essential element of grand Floridian plans is the lanai, a covered and protected private space where pools, fountains, and other water features are likely to be found. Perfect for family activities or for entertaining in any season, the lanai expands the living area and creates a seamless transition to the outdoors.

Among the new Southern house plans, only Floridians are consistently asymmetrical, with offset entries sheltered from the sun by arches, porches, or porticos. Varied rooflines, courtyards, and hard-wearing exterior materials such as stucco are common features. Influenced by architecture from around the world, Floridian plans are at home in any region and particularly well suited to the warm climates of the South.

This beach house is clearly Floridian, with its offset entry, hipped roofs, and sun-reflecting colors. Colonial touches like the fanlights, sidelights, multipaned windows and clapboard siding are pure Southern inspiration.

**Above: Historic details called out in white, a double-height porch, and Southern-style roofs all provide a period look to this thoroughly modern home.**

# Southerness

The South has a charm that permeates daily life. From their regional foods to their balmy weather to their architecture, Southerners have an enviable lifestyle, and their inviting homes are at the center of that delightful culture. There is something equally special about a new Southern home that appears to be steeped in generations of tradition, yet invites all the activities of 21st Century family life.

What is it exactly that makes a new home feel Southern? According to architects and house designers, it is the appearance of tradition, the sense that a new home has been rooted in its site for years, which recreates the type of charm found in homes of the Old South.

Muse Architects of Washington, D.C., are well known for the houses they design throughout the South. Principal William Kirwan has some advice about what gives a new house old Southern charm.

In his practice, Kirwan says he uses contextual architecture to make a new house look established. "Derive the influence for design from the surroundings," he said. "When in the context of the local area, a traditional design response is appropriate. Images of a Southern house include big, long porches, two-story porches, or porticos supported on columns."

Homes designed today can be interpreted in a traditional manner and still function well for a modern lifestyle. "There is definitely a climatic influence in Southern home architecture," Kirwan said. "Porches and overhangs are deeper than would be found in other locations. In the South the object is to keep the heat out."

But deep overhangs and vast porches can create darker spaces than is desired by contemporary homeowners. For the homes he designs, Kirwan will frequently include skylights in porch roofs to brighten the space. He finds that porch skylights best complement a plan when they are designed to work within the geometry of the house. Sometimes a balustrade in front of a flat-roofed porch can hide a skylight. Other times the skylights are visible and seamlessly integrated into the Southern look of the house.

There are other design strategies that evoke the architecture of the Old South. "In colder places, rooms were grouped around a central hearth. But in the South, narrow houses were common, some only a single room wide, to provide the most air flow and keep the rooms cool," Kirwan said.

Southern roof styles are heavily influenced by Greek Revival architecture. Roofs are low-pitched so that heat cannot build up inside.

Roofs get shallower in more Southern locales and as the average temperatures rise.

To get a Southern look in a new home, Kirwan suggests the best investments are in exterior details like porches, tall windows, painted clapboard siding, and painted or unpainted brick. Pediments over the front door are good details, as are balustrades. His advice is to look to the site, its surroundings, and the local community for context and also to identify a Southern tradition that can guide the plans for a new home that looks old.

**Right: Columns flanking this front door create a traditional entryway. For details on this home, see page 82.**

# Southern Style

**Above, top right and bottom: Relaxing on the porch is a Southern institution. Symmetrical columns and ornamental railings in front, along with tall windows behind are elements that give deep Southern porches their inviting and enduring qualities, regardless of the house style or location.**

Southern inspiration is all about creating a house with a timeless air. Respecting the guidelines of a specific style such as Georgian, Federalist, Greek Revival, or Floridian requires working within time-tested design parameters, but that does not mean a new home must be an exact replica of an old plan.

On the exterior, the overall shape might mimic the long narrow houses of the past, but be expanded to include more rooms and more spacious interiors. Exterior materials could appear similar to historic Southern homes, but be hard-wearing, maintenance-free modern alternatives.

Old houses tend to evolve over time, and one way to make a new house look like it has been around for generations is to incorporate areas that seem to be additions, like lower wings on a Georgian design, or a screened porch behind a Federalist style home. When the volumes of these "additions" have distinct rooflines, the sense of an enduring homestead is enhanced.

Details are important in creating the image of a style. When windows and columns and trim are crafted to look like period details, they establish an historic look. And new materials manufactured and produced to look old can boost the authentic appearance.

Old houses were "designed" on all sides, not just the front. The most authentic-looking house plans will have Southern-inspired details on all facades. Interiors and even the garden will have the same level of attention to detail, even when new home spaces are larger or more open than in times past to suit the needs of the modern homeowner.

Southern design is all about charm and character. Modern homes that are sensitive to place and tradition will be stylishly timeless, and are sure to set the tone for future generations of Southern inspiration.

# Southern Style

Beautiful flooring marks a
grand Southern entry.

# Present Perfect

The architectural vocabulary of the Old South takes a new twist as it extends to interior spaces. Open plans and large rooms are the norm for new home plans, and interiors are most often light-filled and airy, thanks to many tall windows. In Southern-themed interiors, cherished details are recreated to provide interiors that feel authentic. Arched openings, doorways, and windows are some of the classically inspired touches regularly appearing in new homes modeled on Colonial-era residences. Elegant and elaborate or simple and sophisticated, moldings are applied as generously today as in homes of the Old South. The imperfections of age in both grand and modest homes can add a look of stability to new interiors; worn finishes and luscious patinas are often speci-

fied to indicate years of use in modern Southern homes.

Entries are important. They set the stage for the whole house. Their role is to identify the transition from the outdoors in, so most Southern entrances include lots of little windows near the front door, either as a fanlight or transom above, or as sidelights. Natural flooring materials like wood or stone are authentic options for the foyer that speaks across centuries.

Reviving the past inside a Southern-inspired home depends on only a few features. Grand staircases and columns between living spaces are important Southern accents. Paneled wood doors, bead-board wall treatments, multipaned windows and interior doors, and natural materials throughout all add to the sense that a home has been around for a long time. Let color, form, furniture, and fabric subtly infuse a fresh sense of style.

**Top Left: Decorative flourishes, curved rooms, and applied ceiling curves are all Federalist features that endure.**
**Top Right: While the execution varies dramatically, arched openings and sweeping staircases declare the Southern inspiration in both of these interior spaces.**

## Down South

**Above: An outdoor room and a Southern-style walled garden are natural retreats that offer additional living space in good weather.**

Site planning, and thus town planning, in Southern cities has some revered models. Places like Charleston have cast the mold for many smart growth strategies of cities around the nation. Constricted by water boundaries, Charleston was forced to develop a unique Southern style of architecture that would provide cooling for its residents. Long, narrow homes, often a single room wide, lined the streets

and grilled balconies overhung the sidewalks to allow air to flow through the spaces from an adjacent narrow garden that also served the house next door. Some smaller houses in Charleston had the garden to the rear, and would let the air flow through "shotgun-" style.

In Savannah, the homes were generally more square in shape, but they raised the main living spaces above the first floor to improve air circulation. Gardens again helped provide space for air to move inside.

Gardens are still integral to the most successful Southern homes. The boxwoods and magnolias of old gardens are still popular for newer homes. But while once the Southern garden was just a place to stroll, today the garden has become an extension of the house. Even diminutive outdoor rooms provide seamless transitions from the interior, and the agreeable climate means they can be used most of the year. ■

**Archways, walls, gates, hedges, and trees help to define and separate each space.**

# Historic Grandeur

*This home boasts all the splendor of historic Southern architecture*

With its symmetrical design, four prominent chimneys, a pediment-capped portico, and grand columns, this brick Colonial speaks with a Southern accent. Sidelights and a fanlight invitingly surround the front door, and a second door above leads to a small balcony. Multipaned tall windows on the front facade are all double hung to let in lots of light. Hipped roofs, long window shutters, a generous front porch, ornamented capitals, and keystone quoins all add to the look of permanence this home exudes, as though it has been in the family for generations.

Inside, the floor plan is anything but old fashioned. From the front door there is a view of the living areas, along with a glimpse of a rear porch and optional pool. The generous foyer leads to a sunken living room, and both spaces are two-story. Grand columns separate the living areas, and many interior details are rendered in warm, rich woods. A fireplace and extensive built-ins for art, books, and entertainment media in the living room are just some of the features that make this home so welcoming.

**Above: The two-story columns and symmetrical facade are hallmarks of classic Southern design.**

**Above: The rear verandah is a perfect spot to sit or swim in the optional pool. Right: Elegant interior spaces have high ceilings and partial walls to let in light and add drama to spaces in the open areas, like the sunken living room.**

An inviting kitchen can be glimpsed to the left of the living room, with more built-ins in warm tones of wood. In addition to a spacious dining room, there is a bay area for eating in the kitchen, along with an outdoor veranda with its own grill and bar. The protected veranda is the perfect spot to sit in privacy, yet it provides visual access to the pool and the back porch.

The right wing is a luxurious retreat, where the master bedroom suite is located with its own sitting room, a two-sided fireplace, and a wing-shaped bath and dressing area with a large tub and private access to the pool. Beyond the study is a guest room and another bath. A double staircase leads upstairs where two large bedrooms each have their own bath and study area. An ornamental iron railing along the second-floor balcony allows the intended library area to be seen from the foyer below. ■

Right: The row of columns and change in ceiling height help set the kitchen and breakfast area apart from the living room. Below: The living room features a large hearth and a sitting area on the balcony above.

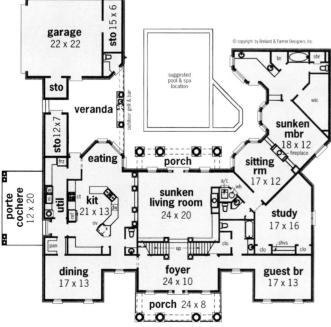

A pro-style range and an angled serving bar help make this kitchen sing.

**plan# HPK1100001**

Style: SOUTHERN COLONIAL
First Floor: 3,439 sq. ft.
Second Floor: 803 sq. ft.
Total: 4,242 sq. ft.
Bedrooms: 4
Bathrooms: 4 + 3 Half Baths
Width: 95' - 0"
Depth: 90' - 0"
Foundation: Slab, Unfinished Basement, Crawlspace

**search online @ eplans.com**

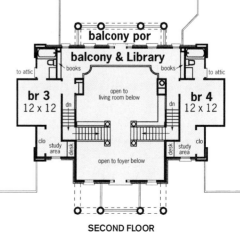

© copyright by Breland & Farmer Designers, Inc.

garage
22 x 22

sto 15 x 6

sto

veranda

sto 12 x 7

outdoor grill & bar

suggested pool & spa location

eating

porch

sunken mbr
18 x 12

fireplace

sitting rm
17 x 12

wic

lin

shr

porte cochere
12 x 20

util

kit
21 x 13

sunken living room
24 x 20

study
17 x 16

a/c
wh

dining
17 x 13

foyer
24 x 10

guest br
17 x 13

porch 24 x 8

**FIRST FLOOR**

balcony por

balcony & Library

to attic

books

br 3
12 x 12

open to living room below

br 4
12 x 12

to attic

books

clo

study area

desk

dn

dn

study area

desk

clo

open to foyer below

**SECOND FLOOR**

# Charming Tradition

*Colonial designs are timeless examples of grand Southern architecture*

In the best tradition of Georgian Colonial architecture, this home design is based on symmetry. Identical wings flank the main part of the house, and an elegant entryway, with its pediment and large columns, is an integral part of its gracious Southern style.

**Above:** This symmetrical brick facade exudes elegance and luxury, evident in the stately columns and twin chimneys. **Left:** Intricate details like the mantel and trim in the living room add beauty and charm to this home.

Interior spaces of this four-bedroom home are spacious and have been planned to keep private quarters separated from the more public living areas. The entry opens to the living room on the left and also leads to a family room in the back. A formal dining room off the kitchen is easily accessed from the kitchen, as well. A seamless flow from kitchen to breakfast area to family room makes this partially open space multifunctional and perfect for family gatherings or entertaining large crowds.

Grand Palladian windows, with their arches and numerous panes, overlook the

**Above: The family room features a Palladian window overlooking the backyard. Left: The spacious master bedroom enjoys sunlit views accented by the heightened ceiling.**

The island kitchen offers classic charm as well as modern convenience.

GARAGE
21'0"X23'0"

©William E. Poole Designs

TERRACE

STORAGE

WASH / DRY UTILITY

SINK

BEDROOM 4
11'0"X13'0"

BATH 3

PORCH

TUB/SHWR

BROOM

FAMILY ROOM
18'0"X19'0"
VAULTED TRAY
CEILING

BOOKCASE

BREAKFAST
AREA
14'6"X12'0"

S.U.

OVENS

KITCHEN
16'0"X13'0"

SINK

SINK

DORIC COLUMNS

ENTERTAINMENT CENTER

MASTER BEDROOM
15'0"X19'0"

MASTER BATH

SHWR

WHIRLPOOL TUB

W.C

LINEN

WARDROBE

REFRIG

PANTRY

DESK

LIVING ROOM
18'6"X13'0"

POWDER
ROOM

W.C

FOYER

BEDROOM 3
15'6"X13'0"

BEDROOM 2
16'0"X13'8"

DINING ROOM
16'0"X14'0"

BATH 2

LINEN

W.C

PORTICO

**ptan # HPK1100002**

Style: **GEORGIAN**
Square Footage: **3,136**
Bedrooms: **4**
Bathrooms: **3½**
Width: **80' - 6"**
Depth: **72' - 4"**
Foundation: **Crawlspace**

search online @ eplans.com

rear gardens from the family room and master bedroom. A guest room is located to the back of the home, in the left wing, affording privacy to overnight visitors. Two fireplaces, lots of built-ins, a kitchen island, and a porch nestled along the breakfast area and family room are just a few of the amenities that make this Southern home a standout design. ■

# Plantations and Farmhouses

Many elegant plantation homes were built in the American South before the Civil War. Large plantations were scattered about the region, from Maryland down to Florida. These large estates often boasted a grand manor house, numerous outbuildings, and many slaves, and became the benchmark for what many consider Southern architecture. But smaller family-oriented farms were just as likely to have distinctive homes—ones that may not share the same scale as the larger plantations, but carry on the legacy of Southern design.

While plantation homes can be almost any style of architecture, the historical image is one of a rambling farmhouse, with long, low lines and lots of porches with deep over-hangs. Here the homeowner and his guests can settle on a hot sunny afternoon to sip their drinks and find some relief from the heat. Materials are elegant but sturdy, and floor plans are intended to function smoothly.

Southern farmhouses and plantation homes built today are most recognized by their deep windows that let in light and breezes, and also by their high porch roofs, which are often two stories and supported on ornamented columns. Colonial plantation homes moved the kitchen out of the house to a separate building in an attempt to manage the heat generated by cooking. But the modern plantation home centers life on the kitchen and family room, bringing everyone together, as seen in the many outstanding designs presented in this chapter. ■

This impressive home, found on page 37, carries distinct Southern charm.

# Farmhouse Culture
*Plantation homes are an enduring Southern tradition*

A Southern-style mansion of graceful proportions, this plantation home would be equally suited to a vast country estate as to a large in-town site. In either location it will provide all the space needed for genteel entertaining and a refined lifestyle. A long, generally low house profile, roofs with overhangs, and a soaring front porch with magnificent columns are design features in keeping with the grand farmhouse tradition of the Old South.

**Above: Long, low lines identify the plantation-style homes of the Old South. This new home borrows the proportions of the past, along with grand ornaments such as the two-story columns and a pediment above the front porch.**

**Above: The octagonal library offers panoramic views. Left: Luxurious curves and a staircase create a welcoming entry.**

This luxurious plantation home is sheltered from the summer sun by its two-story entry portico, yet allows lots of light inside. The bright and welcoming foyer focuses on an oval gallery immediately beyond, delineated by a curved railing above and a spiral staircase that winds its way down. A vast ceiling medallion and chandelier complete the picture-perfect gallery.

An octagonal library at the front of the house promises views in almost every direction and plenty of daylight for reading. A formal dining room, music room, and hearth room all provide places for receiving visitors. The vast kitchen and grand space in the rear are perfect for lavish entertaining. To the rear, an expansive deck with a covered porch on one side and a pampering spa at the other guarantee hours of relaxation. The main-floor master suite is extensive and very private. Upstairs are three more bedrooms, one devoted to an elegant guest suite. ■

Left: The breakfast nook models its shape in part on the library, creating a pleasing rhythm throughout the house.
Below: The rear of the home boasts plenty of outdoor space, such as a ground-level patio and a main-level porch.

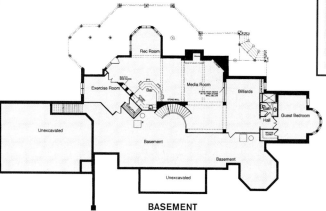

**plan#** HPK1100003

Style: **PLANTATION**
First Floor: 4,011 sq. ft.
Second Floor: 2,198 sq. ft.
Total: 6,209 sq. ft.
Bedrooms: 4
Bathrooms: 3½ + ½
Width: 136' - 0"
Depth: 69' - 2"
Foundation: Unfinished
Walkout Basement

search online @ eplans.com

Above: Rosy woods and a decorative backsplash lend Italian Country style to the kitchen.

**BASEMENT**

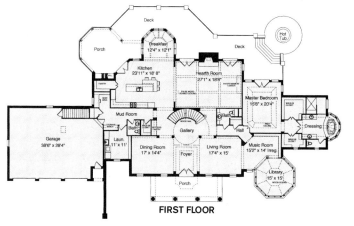

**FIRST FLOOR**

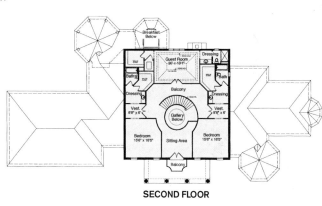

**SECOND FLOOR**

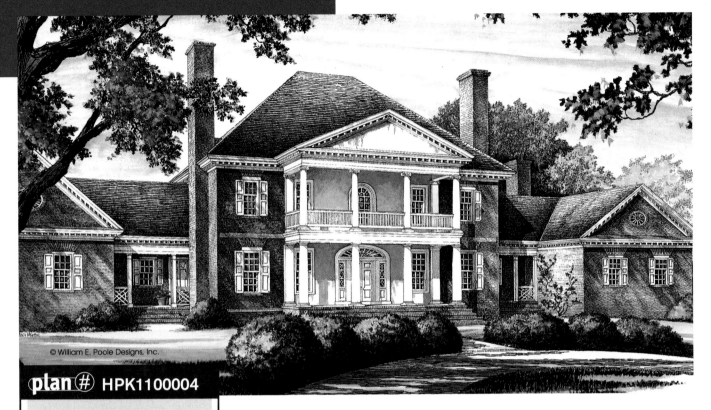

© William E. Poole Designs, Inc.

## plan# HPK1100004

**Style: PLANTATION**
First Floor: 3,635 sq. ft.
Second Floor: 1,357 sq. ft.
Total: 4,992 sq. ft.
Bonus Space: 759 sq. ft.
Bedrooms: 4
Bathrooms: 4½ + ½
Width: 121' - 6"
Depth: 60' - 4"
Foundation: Unfinished
Basement, Crawlspace

**search online @ eplans.com**

**The grandeur of this Southern estate** belies the practical floor plan within. An elegant foyer joins the dining room and oversized living room—both with fireplaces—to welcome guests. The left wing comprises a gourmet kitchen with a walk-in pantry, two powder rooms, and a utility area featuring a mudroom and a separate entrance. The two-story family room, with porch access and a fireplace, is central; the right wing is devoted to a luxurious master suite and a private study, each with a fireplace. An expansive upper level includes three family suites, a balcony overlook, and future space for a fifth bedroom and bath, as well as a game room.

**FIRST FLOOR**

**SECOND FLOOR**

© William E. Poole Designs, Inc.

## plan# HPK1100005

**Style: PLANTATION**
First Floor: 2,913 sq. ft.
Second Floor: 1,380 sq. ft.
Total: 4,293 sq. ft.
Bonus Space: 905 sq. ft.
Bedrooms: 4
Bathrooms: 4½
Width: 88' - 4"
Depth: 100' - 8"
Foundation: Crawlspace

**search online @ eplans.com**

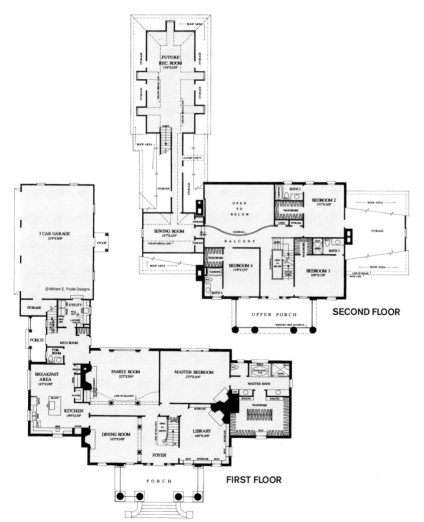

FIRST FLOOR

SECOND FLOOR

**A classic Southern beauty,** grand columns frame the regal entry of this two-story Plantation home. Once inside, the family living spaces are distinguished by decorative interior columns. The L-shaped kitchen easily serves the nearby dining and family rooms. Four fireplaces are peppered throughout the first floor, with one in the master bedroom as a romantic added bonus. Upstairs, three additional family bedrooms each boast a walk-in closet and a full bath. A sewing room and future rec room above the garage complete this plan.

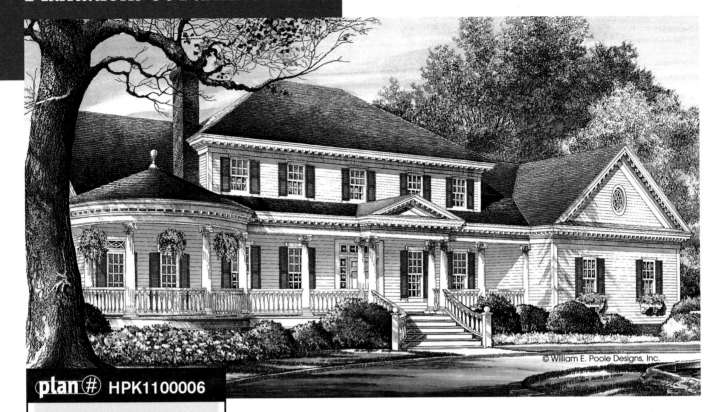

© William E. Poole Designs, Inc.

## plan # HPK1100006

**Style: FARMHOUSE**
First Floor: 2,442 sq. ft.
Second Floor: 1,286 sq. ft.
Total: 3,728 sq. ft.
Bonus Space: 681 sq. ft.
Bedrooms: 4
Bathrooms: 3½ + ½
Width: 84' - 8"
Depth: 60' - 0"
Foundation: Crawlspace

**search online @ eplans.com**

**With a gazebo-style covered porch** and careful exterior details, you can't help but imagine tea parties, porch swings, and lazy summer evenings. Inside, a living room/library will comfort with its fireplace and built-ins. The family room is graced with a fireplace and a curved, two-story ceiling with an overlook above. The master bedroom is a private retreat with a lovely bath, twin walk-in closets, and rear-porch access. Upstairs, three bedrooms with sizable closets—one bedroom would make an excellent guest suite or alternate master suite—share access to expandable space.

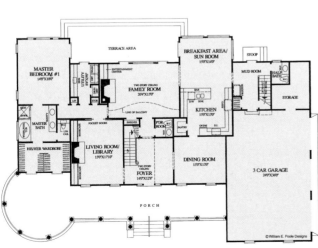

**FIRST FLOOR**

**SECOND FLOOR**

**REAR EXTERIOR**

**Finely crafted porches**—front, side, and rear—make this home a classic in traditional Southern living. Past the large French doors, the impressive foyer is flanked by the formal living and dining rooms. Beyond the stair is a vaulted great room with an expanse of windows, a fireplace, and built-in bookcases. From here, the breakfast room and kitchen are easily accessible and open to a private side porch. The master suite provides a large bath, two spacious closets, and a fireplace. The second floor contains three bedrooms with private bath access and a playroom.

**plan # HPK1100007**

**Style: PLANTATION**
**First Floor: 2,380 sq. ft.**
**Second Floor: 1,295 sq. ft.**
**Total: 3,675 sq. ft.**
**Bedrooms: 4**
**Bathrooms: 3½**
**Width: 77' - 4"**
**Depth: 58' - 4"**
**Foundation: Walkout Basement**

**search online @ eplans.com**

QUOTE ONE®

**FIRST FLOOR**

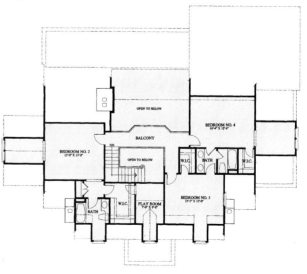

**SECOND FLOOR**

## plan# HPK1100008

**Style: FARMHOUSE**
First Floor: 1,995 sq. ft.
Second Floor: 1,062 sq. ft.
Total: 3,057 sq. ft.
Bonus Space: 459 sq. ft.
Bedrooms: 4
Bathrooms: 3½
Width: 71' - 0"
Depth: 57' - 4"
Foundation: Unfinished Basement

**search online @ eplans.com**

**Wood siding, muntin window dormers,** and a double-decker porch exemplify Southern Country style in this welcoming plan. Slide off your porch swing and enter through the foyer, flanked by the bayed living room and dining room. The family room flows effortlessly into the breakfast area and the kitchen, complete with an island. The master bedroom wows with a closet designed for a true clotheshorse. Three upstairs bedrooms enjoy access to the upper porch and space for a future recreation room.

FIRST FLOOR

SECOND FLOOR

© William E. Poole Designs, Inc.

**plan# HPK1100009**

**Style: FARMHOUSE**
**First Floor:** 1,913 sq. ft.
**Second Floor:** 997 sq. ft.
**Total:** 2,910 sq. ft.
**Bonus Space:** 377 sq. ft.
**Bedrooms:** 4
**Bathrooms:** 3½
**Width:** 63' - 0"
**Depth:** 59' - 4"
**Foundation:** Crawlspace, Unfinished Basement

**search online @ eplans.com**

**REAR EXTERIOR**

**SECOND FLOOR**

**FIRST FLOOR**

**This enchanting farmhouse** brings the past to life with plenty of modern amenities. An open-flow kitchen/breakfast area and family room combination is the heart of the home, opening up to the screened porch and enjoying the warmth of a fireplace. For more formal occasions, the foyer is flanked by a living room on the left and a dining room on the right. An elegant master bedroom, complete with a super-size walk-in closet, is tucked away quietly behind the garage. Three more bedrooms reside upstairs, along with two full baths and a future recreation room.

© William E. Poole Designs, Inc.

## plan# HPK1100010

**Style: FARMHOUSE**

**First Floor:** 2,191 sq. ft.

**Second Floor:** 1,220 sq. ft.

**Total:** 3,411 sq. ft.

**Bonus Space:** 280 sq. ft.

**Bedrooms:** 4

**Bathrooms:** 3½

**Width:** 75' - 8"

**Depth:** 54' - 4"

**Foundation:** Crawlspace, Unfinished Basement

**search online @ eplans.com**

**This Colonial farmhouse will be the showpiece** of your neighborhood. Come in from the wide front porch through French doors topped by a sunburst window. Continue past the formal dining and living rooms to a columned gallery and a large family room with a focal fireplace. The kitchen astounds with a unique layout, an island, and abundant counter and cabinet space. The master bath balances luxury with efficiency. Three upstairs bedrooms enjoy amenities such as dormer windows or walk-in closets. Bonus space is ready for expansion as your needs change.

**FIRST FLOOR**

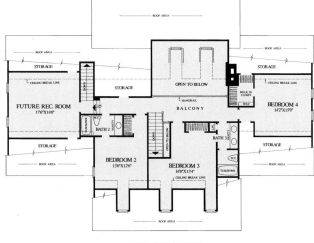

**SECOND FLOOR**

© William E. Poole Designs, Inc.

**Three petite dormers top a welcoming** covered porch and add a touch of grace to an already beautiful home. Inside, the foyer opens to the left to a formal dining room, which in turn has easy access to the efficient kitchen. Here, a pantry and a snack bar in the breakfast area make meal preparations a delight. The nearby spacious family room features a fireplace, built-in bookshelves, and outdoor access. Located away from the master suite for privacy, two family bedrooms pamper with private baths and walk-in closets. On the other end of the home, the master suite provides luxury via a huge walk-in closet, whirlpool tub, and corner shower with a seat. An optional second floor features a fourth bedroom in private splendor with its own bath and access to a recreation room complete with a second fireplace.

**plan# HPK1100011**

Style: **FARMHOUSE**
Square Footage: **2,215**
Bedrooms: **3**
Bathrooms: **3**
Width: **69' - 10"**
Depth: **62' - 6"**
Foundation: **Crawlspace, Unfinished Basement**

search online @ eplans.com

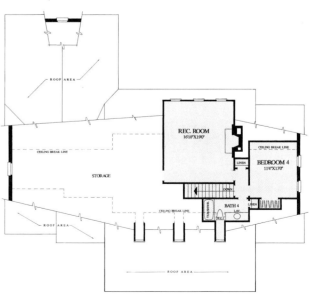

PHOTO COURTESY OF: WILLIAM E. POOLE DESIGNS, INC. PHOTO BY STEVE DIGGS. THIS HOME AS SHOWN IN THE PHOTOGRAPH MAY DIFFER FROM THE ACTUAL BLUEPRINTS.

**plan# HPK1100012**

**Style: FARMHOUSE**
First Floor: 1,927 sq. ft.
Second Floor: 879 sq. ft.
Total: 2,806 sq. ft.
Bonus Space: 459 sq. ft.
Bedrooms: 4
Bathrooms: 3½
Width: 71' - 0"
Depth: 53' - 0"
Foundation: Crawlspace

search online @ eplans.com

**This charming Southern plantation home** packs quite a punch in 2,800 square feet! The elegant foyer is flanked by the formal dining room and the living room. To the rear, the family room enjoys a fireplace and expansive view of the outdoors. An archway leads to the breakfast area and on to the island kitchen. The luxurious master suite is tucked away for privacy behind the two-car garage. Three additional bedrooms rest on the second floor where they share two full baths. Space above the garage is available for future development.

**FIRST FLOOR**

**SECOND FLOOR**

© William E. Poole Designs, Inc.

**plan # HPK1100013**

**This charming farmhouse** starts out with a welcoming front porch lined with columns. Inside, the foyer opens to the right to the formal dining room. At the rear of the home, a two-story great room provides a fireplace, built-ins, and direct access to the backyard. The nearby kitchen is complete with a walk-in pantry and an adjacent breakfast area. The first-floor master suite offers a large walk-in closet and a pampering bath. Upstairs, two family bedrooms share a hall bath.

Style: **FARMHOUSE**
First Floor: 1,556 sq. ft.
Second Floor: 623 sq. ft.
Total: 2,179 sq. ft.
Bonus Space: 368 sq. ft.
Bedrooms: 3
Bathrooms: 2½
Width: 73' - 4"
Depth: 41' - 4"
Foundation: Crawlspace, Finished Basement

**search online @ eplans.com**

FIRST FLOOR

SECOND FLOOR

# Plantations & Farmhouses

© William E. Poole Designs, Inc.

## plan# HPK1100014

Style: **FARMHOUSE**
First Floor: 2,014 sq. ft.
Second Floor: 976 sq. ft.
Total: 2,990 sq. ft.
Bonus Space: 390 sq. ft.
Bedrooms: 4
Bathrooms: 3½
Width: 73' - 9"
Depth: 55' - 5"
Foundation: Crawlspace,
Unfinished Basement

search online @ eplans.com

**Wide steps lead up to a covered front porch,** inviting one to step inside and appreciate the welcome expressed by this fine four-bedroom home. The two-story foyer is flanked by the formal dining room to the left and the formal living room to the right. A pocket door leads from the living room into the spacious family room, where a fireplace waits to warm cool fall evenings. The L-shaped island kitchen offers an adjacent breakfast area, as well as a pantry and built-in desk. The first-floor master suite is designed to pamper, with a huge walk-in closet, a whirlpool tub, corner shower, and private outdoor access. Upstairs, three family bedrooms, two full baths, and a large future recreation room complete the plan.

FIRST FLOOR

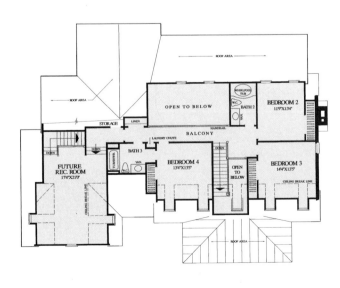

© WILLIAM E POOLE DESIGNS, INC.

**This home is an absolute dream** when it comes to living space! Whether formal or casual, there's a room for every occasion. The foyer opens to the formal dining room on the left; straight ahead lies the magnificent hearth-warmed living room. The island kitchen opens not only to a breakfast nook, but to a huge family/sunroom surrounded by two walls of windows! The right wing of the plan holds the sleeping quarters—two family bedrooms sharing a bath, and a majestic master suite. The second floor holds an abundance of expandable space.

## plan# HPK1100015

Style: **FARMHOUSE**
Square Footage: **2,777**
Bonus Space: **424 sq. ft.**
Bedrooms: **3**
Bathrooms: **2½**
Width: **75' - 6"**
Depth: **60' - 2"**
Foundation: **Crawlspace, Unfinished Basement**

**search online @ eplans.com**

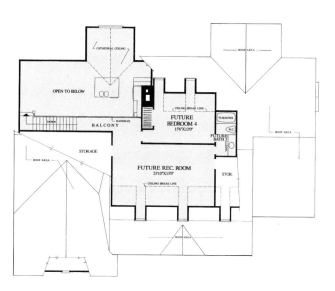

**REAR EXTERIOR**

# Plantations & Farmhouses

## plan# HPK1100016

**Style: FARMHOUSE**
Square Footage: 2,151
Bonus Space: 814 sq. ft.
Bedrooms: 3
Bathrooms: 2
Width: 61' - 0"
Depth: 55' - 8"
Foundation: Crawlspace, Unfinished Basement

**search online @ eplans.com**

**Country flavor is well established** on this fine three-bedroom home. The covered front porch welcomes friends and family alike to the foyer, where the formal dining room opens off to the left. The vaulted ceiling in the great room enhances the warmth of the fireplace and the wall of windows. An efficient kitchen works well with the bayed breakfast area. The secluded master suite offers a walk-in closet and a lavish bath; on the other side of the home, two family bedrooms share a full bath. Upstairs, an optional fourth bedroom is available for guests or in-laws and provides access to a large recreation room.

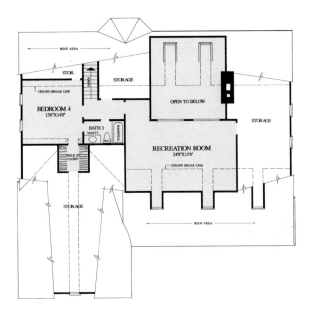

**ptan(#) HPK1100017**

Style: **PLANTATION**
First Floor: 2,142 sq. ft.
Second Floor: 960 sq. ft.
Total: 3,102 sq. ft.
Bonus Space: 327 sq. ft.
Bedrooms: 4
Bathrooms: 3½
Width: 75' - 8"
Depth: 53' - 0"
Foundation: Crawlspace

search online @ eplans.com

**Imagine driving up to this cottage** beauty at the end of a long week. The long wraparound porch, hipped rooflines, and shuttered windows will transport you. Inside, the foyer is flanked by a living room on the left and a formal dining room on the right. Across the gallery hall, the hearth-warmed family room will surely become the hub of the home. To the right, the spacious kitchen boasts a worktop island counter, ample pantry space, and a breakfast area. A short hallway opens to the utility room and the two-car garage. The master suite takes up the entire left wing of the home, enjoying an elegant private bath and a walk-in closet that goes on and on. Upstairs, three more bedrooms reside, sharing two full baths. Expandable future space awaits on the right.

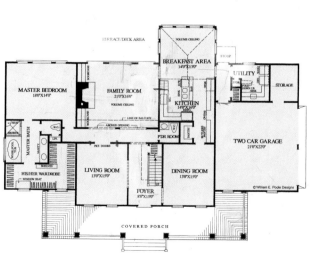

**FIRST FLOOR**

**SECOND FLOOR**

# Plantations & Farmhouses

## plan# HPK1100018

**Style: FARMHOUSE**
**Square Footage: 2,172**
**Bedrooms: 3**
**Bathrooms: 2**
**Width: 79' - 0"**
**Depth: 47' - 0"**
**Foundation: Crawlspace, Slab**

**search online @ eplans.com**

**The simplicity of the ranch lifestyle** is indicated in every detail of this charming country design. Front and rear verandas along with earthy materials combine to give the exterior of this home a true land-lover's look. A central fireplace warms the cathedral-enhanced space of the formal great room. The casual kitchen area features an island workstation overlooking the rear veranda. The master suite is a sumptuous retreat with a sitting area, private bath, and walk-in closet. Two additional bedrooms share a full hall bath.

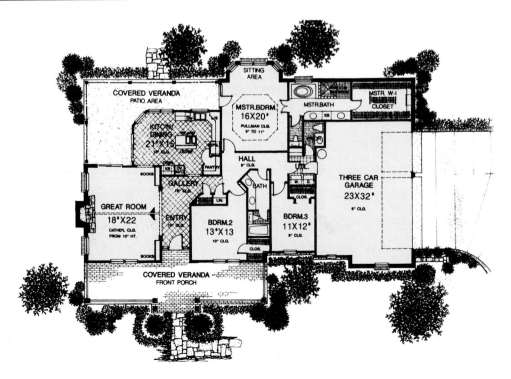

**FIRST FLOOR**

**SECOND FLOOR**

## plan# HPK1100019

**Style: FARMHOUSE**
**First Floor:** 1,819 sq. ft.
**Second Floor:** 638 sq. ft.
**Total:** 2,457 sq. ft.
**Bonus Space:** 385 sq. ft.
**Bedrooms:** 3
**Bathrooms:** 2½
**Width:** 47' - 4"
**Depth:** 82' - 8"
**Foundation: Crawlspace,**
**Unfinished Basement**

**search online @ eplans.com**

**Graceful dormers top a welcoming** covered porch that is enhanced by Victorian details on this fine three-bedroom home. Inside, the foyer leads past the formal dining room back to the spacious two-story great room. Here, a fireplace, built-ins, and outdoor access make any gathering special. The nearby kitchen features a work island, a pantry, a serving bar, and an adjacent bayed breakfast area. Located on the first floor for privacy, the master suite is designed to pamper. Upstairs, two family bedrooms share a hall bath. Note the bonus space above the two-car garage.

# Plantations & Farmhouses

© WILLIAM E POOLE DESIGNS, INC.

## plan# HPK1100020

**Style: FARMHOUSE**
First Floor: 1,832 sq. ft.
Second Floor: 574 sq. ft.
Total: 2,406 sq. ft.
Bonus Space: 410 sq. ft.
Bedrooms: 4
Bathrooms: 3
Width: 77' - 10"
Depth: 41' - 4"
Foundation: Crawlspace

**search online @ eplans.com**

**This farmhouse style welcomes you** with shuttered windows and doorway, and covered front and side porch. An open floor plan with an inside balcony creates a feeling of expansiveness. French doors; a gathering room with fireplace and access to the terrace; a kitchen with pantry, island, and breakfast nook; and everything the inhabitants of the master and one family bedroom will ever need round out the highlights of the main floor. Upstairs find bedrooms 3 and 4, a media center, and a great view to below.

**SECOND FLOOR**

**FIRST FLOOR**

© William E. Poole Designs, Inc.

**This Southern coastal cottage radiates** charm and elegance. Step inside from the covered porch and discover a floor plan with practicality and architectural interest. The foyer has a raised ceiling and is partially open to above. The library and great room offer fireplaces and built-in shelves; the great room also provides rear-porch access. The kitchen, featuring an island with a separate sink, is adjacent to the breakfast room and a study with a built-in desk. On the far right, the master bedroom will amaze, with a sumptuous bath and enormous walk-in closet. Three upstairs bedrooms share a loft and recreation room. Convenient storage opportunities make organization easy.

## plan# HPK1100021

**Style: FARMHOUSE**
**First Floor: 2,891 sq. ft.**
**Second Floor: 1,336 sq. ft.**
**Total: 4,227 sq. ft.**
**Bonus Space: 380 sq. ft.**
**Bedrooms: 4**
**Bathrooms: 3½ + ½**
**Width: 90' - 8"**
**Depth: 56' - 4"**
**Foundation: Crawlspace, Unfinished Basement**

**search online @ eplans.com**

**REAR EXTERIOR**

**FIRST FLOOR**

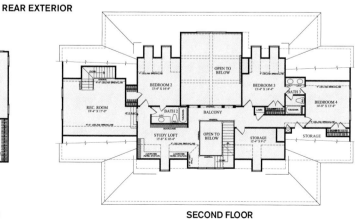

**SECOND FLOOR**

# Plantations & Farmhouses

© William E. Poole Designs, Inc.

## plan# HPK1100022

**Style: FARMHOUSE**
First Floor: 1,694 sq. ft.
Second Floor: 874 sq. ft.
Total: 2,568 sq. ft.
Bonus Space: 440 sq. ft.
Bedrooms: 3
Bathrooms: 3½
Width: 74' - 2"
Depth: 46' - 8"
Foundation: Unfinished
Basement, Crawlspace

**search online @ eplans.com**

**A welcoming front porch** lined by graceful columns introduces this fine farmhouse. Inside, the foyer leads through an elegant arch to the spacious great room, which features a fireplace and built-ins. The formal dining room and sunny breakfast room flank a highly efficient kitchen—complete with a pantry and a serving bar. Located on the first floor for privacy, the master suite is filled with pampering amenities. Upstairs, two large bedrooms have private baths and walk-in closets.

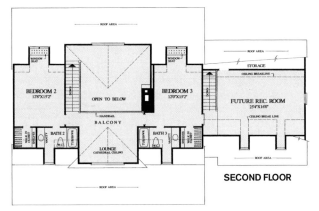

**SECOND FLOOR**

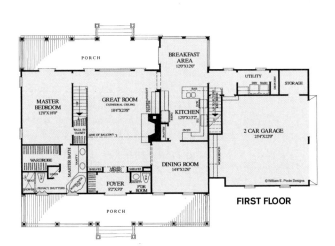

**FIRST FLOOR**

**REAR EXTERIOR**

© 2000 Donald A. Gardner, Inc.

**The small appearance of this country farmhouse** belies the spaciousness within. A large great room is directly beyond the foyer and boasts a fireplace, shelves, a vaulted ceiling, and a door to the rear deck. A bayed breakfast room, located just off the kitchen, looks to a covered breezeway that leads from the house to the garage. The first-floor master bedroom is enhanced with a sitting area, walk-in closet, and full bath with a garden tub and dual sinks. The second floor overlooks the great room and includes three additional bedrooms, one with a cathedral ceiling.

**plan# HPK1100023**

Style: **FARMHOUSE**
First Floor: 1,706 sq. ft.
Second Floor: 776 sq. ft.
Total: 2,482 sq. ft.
Bonus Space: 414 sq. ft.
Bedrooms: 4
Bathrooms: 2½
Width: 54' - 8"
Depth: 43' - 0"
**search online @ eplans.com**

**GARAGE**
22-8 x 22-8

up          storage

DECK

covered
breezeway

SITTING

MASTER
BED RM.
17-8 x 13-4

shelves
(vaulted
ceiling)

fireplace

**GREAT RM.**
18-0 x 19-10

balcony above

BRKFST.
9-0 x 11-2

UTIL.
8-4 x
10-2

w
d
cl

walk-in
closet

KIT.
11-4 x
12-10

master
bath

sto.

pd. rm.

cl

lin.

seat

**FOYER**
10-8 x 8-4
up

**DINING**
16-0 x 11-4

**PORCH**

**FIRST FLOOR**

attic
storage

**BONUS RM.**
14-8 x 23-0

attic
storage

down

great room
below

cl          cl

railing

BED RM.
11-4 x 13-0

down          sto.

BED RM.
11-4 x 11-8

lin.

cl

bath

BED RM.
10-8 x 12-4
(cathedral ceiling)

**SECOND FLOOR**

## plan # HPK1100024

**Style: FARMHOUSE**
First Floor: 1,093 sq. ft.
Second Floor: 576 sq. ft.
Total: 1,669 sq. ft.
Bedrooms: 3
Bathrooms: 2
Width: 52' - 0"
Depth: 46' - 0"
Foundation: Crawlspace

**search online @ eplans.com**

**Here's a great country farmhouse** with a lot of contemporary appeal. The generous use of windows—including two sets of triple muntin windows in the front—adds exciting visual elements to the exterior as well as plenty of natural light to the interior. An impressive tiled entry opens to a two-story great room with a raised hearth and views to the front and side grounds. The U-shaped kitchen conveniently combines with this area and offers a snack counter in addition to a casual dining nook with rear-porch access. The family bedrooms reside on the main level. An expansive master suite with an adjacent study creates a resplendent retreat upstairs, complete with a private balcony, walk-in closet, and bath.

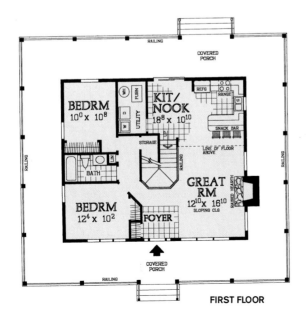

**FIRST FLOOR**

**SECOND FLOOR**

**plan# HPK1100025**

Style: **FARMHOUSE**
Square Footage: 2,090
Bedrooms: 3
Bathrooms: 2½
Width: 84' - 6"
Depth: 64' - 0"
Foundation: Crawlspace

**search online @ eplans.com**

**This classic farmhouse enjoys** a wraparound porch that's perfect for enjoyment of the outdoors. To the rear of the plan, a sun terrace with a spa opens from the master suite and the morning room. A grand great room offers a sloped ceiling and a corner fireplace with a raised hearth. The formal dining room is defined by a low wall and graceful archways set off by decorative columns. The tiled kitchen has a centered island counter with a snack bar and adjoins a laundry area. Two family bedrooms reside to the side of the plan, and each enjoys private access to the covered porch. A secluded master suite nestles in its own wing and features a sitting area with access to the rear terrace and spa.

**plan# HPK1100026**

Style: **FARMHOUSE**
First Floor: 1,439 sq. ft.
Second Floor: 1,419 sq. ft.
Total: 2,858 sq. ft.
Bonus Space: 241 sq. ft.
Bedrooms: 4
Bathrooms: 2½
Width: 63' - 10"
Depth: 40' - 4"
Foundation: Crawlspace,
Unfinished Basement

**search online @ eplans.com**

**Choose from one of two exteriors** for this grand design—a lovely wood-sided farmhouse or a stately brick traditional. Plans include details for both facades. Special moldings and trim add interest to the nine-foot ceilings on the first floor. The dining room features a tray ceiling and is separated from the hearth-warmed living room by decorative columns. A study is secluded behind double doors just off the entry. The centrally located kitchen features a large cooking island, pantry, telephone desk, and ample cupboard and counter space. The family room has a decorative beam ceiling and fireplace. The private master bedroom has a most exquisite bath with His and Hers walk-in closets, a soaking tub, separate shower, and make-up vanity. An optional exercise/sitting room adds 241 square feet to the total. Family bedrooms share a full bath.

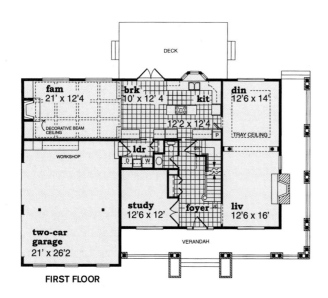

**FIRST FLOOR**

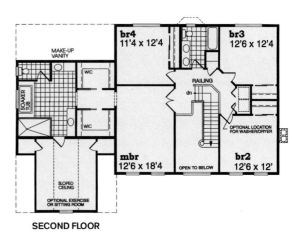

**SECOND FLOOR**

© 1998 Donald A. Gardner Architects, Inc.

**At the front of this farmhouse design,** the master suite includes a sitting bay, two walk-in closets, a door to the front porch, and a compartmented bath with a double-bowl vanity. The formal dining room in the second bay also features a door to the front porch. Access the rear porch from the great room, which opens to the breakfast room under the balcony. On the second floor, three family bedrooms share a bath that has a double-bowl vanity. One of the family bedrooms offers a walk-in closet. A bonus room over the garage can be used as a study or game room.

**plan #** HPK1100027

**Style: FARMHOUSE**
First Floor: 1,614 sq. ft.
Second Floor: 892 sq. ft.
Total: 2,506 sq. ft.
Bonus Space: 341 sq. ft.
Bedrooms: 4
Bathrooms: 2½
Width: 71' - 10"
Depth: 50' - 0"

search online @ eplans.com

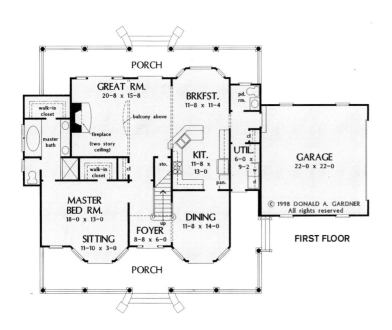

FIRST FLOOR

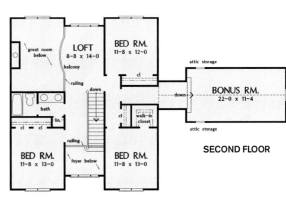

SECOND FLOOR

## plan# HPK1100028

**Style: FARMHOUSE**
First Floor: 2,210 sq. ft.
Second Floor: 1,070 sq. ft.
Total: 3,280 sq. ft.
Bedrooms: 4
Bathrooms: 3½
Width: 60' - 6"
Depth: 58' - 6"
Foundation: Walkout
Basement

**search online @ eplans.com**

**A standing-seam roof,** dormer windows, and a generous front porch enhance the exterior of this welcoming farmhouse. Double doors open to the living room, which has its own fireplace. The family room boasts its own fireplace and French doors that open to a rear deck. The gourmet kitchen features an island cooktop and adjoins a breakfast room brightened by a ribbon of windows. The master suite includes a divided walk-in closet and an angled shower. Upstairs, two additional bedrooms share a full bath that provides two vanities. A third bedroom offers a private bath and a walk-in closet.

**FIRST FLOOR**

**SECOND FLOOR**

**plan # HPK1100029**

Style: **FARMHOUSE**
First Floor: 1,082 sq. ft.
Second Floor: 1,021 sq. ft.
Total: 2,103 sq. ft.
Bedrooms: 4
Bathrooms: 2½
Width: 50' - 0"
Depth: 40' - 0"

**search online @ eplans.com**

**A covered porch invites you** into this country-style home. Handsome bookcases frame the fireplace in the spacious family room. Double doors off the entry provide the family room with added privacy. The kitchen features an island, a lazy Susan, and easy access to a walk-in laundry. The master bedroom features a boxed ceiling and separate entries to a walk-in closet and a pampering bath. The upstairs hall bath is compartmented, allowing maximum usage for today's busy family.

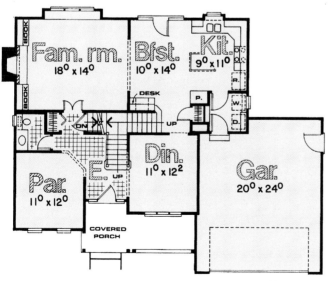

FIRST FLOOR

SECOND FLOOR

**plan # HPK1100030**

**Style: FARMHOUSE**
First Floor: 1,383 sq. ft.
Second Floor: 703 sq. ft.
Total: 2,086 sq. ft.
Bonus Space: 342 sq. ft.
Bedrooms: 4
Bathrooms: 3½
Width: 49' - 0"
Depth: 50' - 0"

**search online @ eplans.com**

**This enchanting farmhouse** looks great in the country, on the waterfront, or on your street! Inside, the foyer is accented by a barrel arch and opens on the right to a formal dining room. An 11-foot ceiling in the living room expands the space, as a warming fireplace makes it feel cozy. The step-saving kitchen easily serves the bayed breakfast nook. In the sumptuous master suite, a sitting area is bathed in natural light, and the walk-in closet is equipped with a built-in dresser. The luxurious bath features dual vanities and a spa tub. Three upstairs bedrooms, one with a private bath, access optional future space, designed to meet your family's needs.

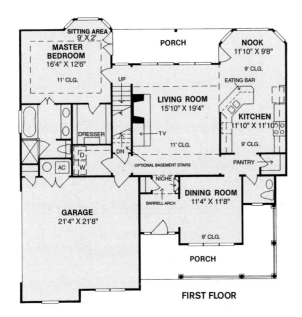

FIRST FLOOR

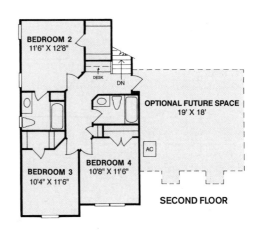

SECOND FLOOR

**plan# HPK1100031**

Style: **FARMHOUSE**
First Floor: 1,771 sq. ft.
Second Floor: 1,235 sq. ft.
Total: 3,006 sq. ft.
Bedrooms: 4
Bathrooms: 3½
Width: 61' - 4"
Depth: 54' - 0"
Foundation: Crawlspace, Slab,
Unfinished Walkout Basement

**search online @ eplans.com**

**Step into the two-story foyer,** where a living room will greet you on the right and a boxed dining room on the left. Further into the plan is a two-story family room with a corner fireplace. The kitchen looks over a bar into the bayed breakfast area, which has rear-door access to the sun deck. The first-floor master bedroom is situated at the rear of the plan for maximum privacy and includes many lavish amenities. The second level presents many unique additions for the whole family. A future media space is perfect for a home theater or perhaps an additional bedroom. Three family bedrooms and two full baths complete the sleeping quarters. A storage space, a loft, and overlooks to the two-story family room and foyer are included in this versatile design.

FIRST FLOOR

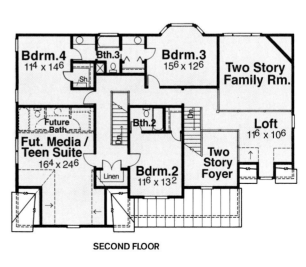

SECOND FLOOR

## plan # HPK1100032

**Style: FARMHOUSE**
First Floor: 1,160 sq. ft.
Second Floor: 1,316 sq. ft.
Total: 2,476 sq. ft.
Bedrooms: 4
Bathrooms: 2½
Width: 52' - 0"
Depth: 44' - 0"
Foundation: Unfinished
Walkout Basement

search online @ eplans.com

**Brick detailing, shingles, and siding** come together to create a refined exterior on this country farmhouse. The foyer is flanked by a dining room and a living room. At the rear of the house is the two-story family room, which is graced with a central fireplace and rear-door access to a sun deck. The kitchen blends into the breakfast area and is provided with backyard views. Storage space, a powder room, and a computer station complete the first floor of this plan. The sleeping quarters upstairs include a lavish master suite—with a full bath and sitting area—three vaulted family bedrooms, another full bath, and a laundry area.

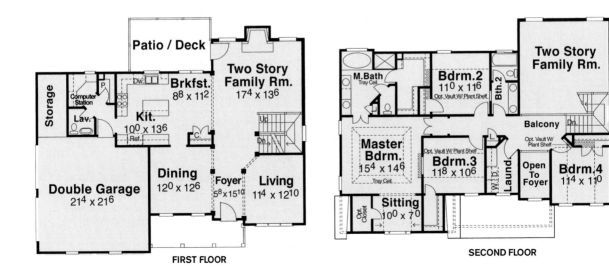

FIRST FLOOR

SECOND FLOOR

**plan# HPK1100033**

Style: **PLANTATION**
First Floor: 2,113 sq. ft.
Second Floor: 2,098 sq. ft.
Total: 4,211 sq. ft.
Bonus Space: 76 sq. ft.
Bedrooms: 5
Bathrooms: 4½
Width: 68' - 6"
Depth: 53' - 0"
Foundation: Slab, Unfinished
Walkout Basement,
Crawlspace

search online @ eplans.com

**This two-story farmhouse has much to offer,** with the most exciting feature being the opulent master suite, which takes up almost the entire width of the upper level. French doors access the large master bedroom, featuring a coffered ceiling. Steps lead to a separate sitting room with a fireplace and sun-filled bay window. His and Hers walk-in closets lead the way to a vaulted private bath with separate vanities and a lavish whirlpool tub. On the first floor, an island kitchen and a bayed breakfast room flow into a two-story family room with a raised-hearth fireplace, built-in shelves, and French-door access to the rear yard.

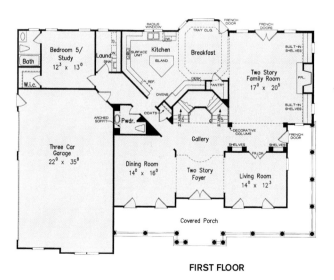

**FIRST FLOOR**

**SECOND FLOOR**

## plan # HPK1100034

**Style: PLANTATION**
First Floor: 2,732 sq. ft.
Second Floor: 2,734 sq. ft.
Total: 5,466 sq. ft.
Bedrooms: 5
Bathrooms: 5½ + ½
Width: 85' - 0"
Depth: 85' - 6"
Foundation: Crawlspace, Slab,
Unfinished Walkout Basement

**search online @ eplans.com**

**A wraparound covered porch** adds plenty of outdoor space to this already impressive home. Built-in cabinets flank the fireplace in the grand room; a fireplace also warms the hearth room. The gourmet kitchen includes an island counter, large walk-in pantry, and serving bar. A secluded home office, with a separate entrance nearby, provides a quiet work place. A front parlor provides even more room for entertaining or relaxing. The master suite dominates the second floor, offering a spacious sitting area with an elegant tray ceiling, a dressing area, and a luxurious bath with two walk-in closets, double vanities, and a raised garden tub. The second floor is also home to an enormous exercise room and three additional bedrooms.

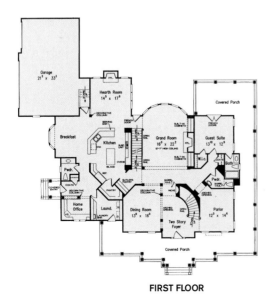

**FIRST FLOOR**

**SECOND FLOOR**

**In this four-bedroom design,** the casual areas are free-flowing, open, and soaring, and the formal areas are secluded and well defined. The two-story foyer with a clerestory window leads to a quiet parlor with a vaulted ceiling and a Palladian window. The formal dining room opens from the foyer through decorative columns and is served by a spacious gourmet kitchen. The family room, defined by columns, has an angled corner hearth and is open to the kitchen and breakfast nook. The master suite is full of interesting angles, from the triangular bedroom and multi-angled walk-in closet to the corner tub in the sumptuous master bath. A nearby den has its own bathroom and could serve as a guest room. Upstairs, two additional bedrooms share a full bath and a balcony hall.

**plan# HPK1100035**

Style: **FARMHOUSE**
First Floor: 2,642 sq. ft.
Second Floor: 603 sq. ft.
Total: 3,245 sq. ft.
Bonus Space: 255 sq. ft.
Bedrooms: 4
Bathrooms: 3½
Width: 80' - 0"
Depth: 61' - 0"
Foundation: Crawlspace

**search online @ eplans.com**

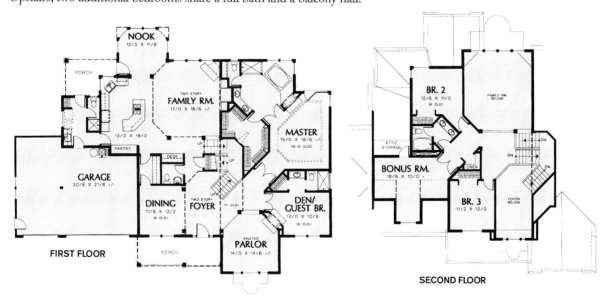

FIRST FLOOR

SECOND FLOOR

## plan # HPK1100036

Style: **FARMHOUSE**
First Floor: 1,570 sq. ft.
Second Floor: 1,630 sq. ft.
Total: 3,200 sq. ft.
Bedrooms: 4
Bathrooms: 3½
Width: 59' - 10"
Depth: 43' - 4"
Foundation: Walkout
Basement

**search online @ eplans.com**

**This classic Americana design** employs wood siding, a variety of window styles, and a detailed front porch. Inside, the large two-story foyer flows into the formal dining room with arched window accents and the living room highlighted by a bay window. A short passage with a wet bar accesses the family room with its wall of windows, French doors, and fireplace. The large breakfast area and open island kitchen are spacious and airy as well as efficient. Upstairs, the master suite's sleeping and sitting rooms feature architectural details including columns, tray ceilings, and a fireplace. The elegant private bath contains a raised oval tub, dual vanities, and a separate shower. A generous walk-in closet is located beyond the bath. Additional bedrooms are complete with closets and a variety of bath combinations.

**REAR EXTERIOR**

**FIRST FLOOR**

**SECOND FLOOR**

A **Palladian window, fish-scale shingles,** and turret-style bays set off this country-style Victorian exterior. Muntin windows and a quintessential wraparound porch dress up an understated theme and introduce an unrestrained floor plan with plenty of bays and niches. An impressive tile entry opens to the formal rooms, which nestle to the left side of the plan and enjoy natural light from an abundance of windows. The turret houses a secluded study on the first floor and provides a sunny bay window for a family bedroom upstairs. The second-floor master suite boasts its own fireplace, a dressing area with a walk-in closet, and a lavish bath with a garden tub and twin vanities. The two-car garage offers space for a workshop or extra storage and leads to a service entrance to the walk-through utility room.

**plan# HPK1100037**

Style: **FARMHOUSE**  L D
First Floor: 1,186 sq. ft.
Second Floor: 988 sq. ft.
Total: 2,174 sq. ft.
Bedrooms: 4
Bathrooms: 2½
Width: 72' - 0"
Depth: 50' - 10"
Foundation: Unfinished Basement

**search online @ eplans.com**

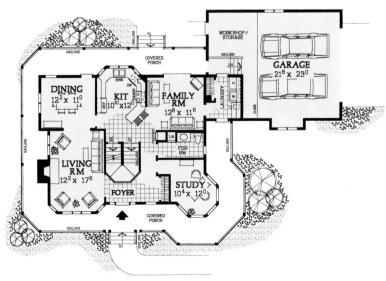

**FIRST FLOOR**

**SECOND FLOOR**

**plan# HPK1100038**

**Style: FARMHOUSE**
First Floor: 1,155 sq. ft.
Second Floor: 1,209 sq. ft.
Total: 2,364 sq. ft.
Bedrooms: 4
Bathrooms: 2½
Width: 46' - 0"
Depth: 36' - 8"
Foundation: Unfinished Basement

**search online @ eplans.com**

**With both farmhouse flavor and Victorian details,** this plan features a wraparound veranda and a bayed area on the first and second floors as well as a turret on the second floor. Inside, the living room's many windows pour light in. The dining area begins with a bay window and is conveniently near the kitchen and breakfast area—also with a bay window. The U-shaped kitchen features an island workstation, ensuring plenty of space for cooking projects. A nearby lavatory is available for guests. The family room has an eye-catching corner-set fireplace. Upstairs, three family bedrooms share a full hall bath, while the master suite has a private bath and balcony, a large walk-in closet, and a sitting alcove, placed within the turret.

**FIRST FLOOR**

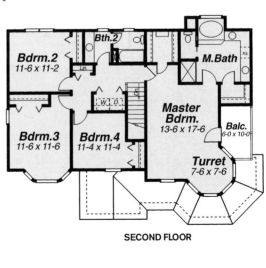

**SECOND FLOOR**

**A touch of Victoriana enhances** the facade of this home: a turret roof over a wraparound porch with turned wood spindles. Special attractions on the first floor include a tray ceiling in the octagonal living room, fireplaces in the country kitchen and the living room, a coffered ceiling in the family room, and double-door access to the cozy den. The master suite, set in the second-floor section of the turret, boasts a coffered ceiling, walk-in closet, and whirlpool tub. Three family bedrooms and a full hall bath join the master suite on the second floor.

**plan# HPK1100039**

**Style: FARMHOUSE**
**First Floor: 1,462 sq. ft.**
**Second Floor: 1,288 sq. ft.**
**Total: 2,750 sq. ft.**
**Bedrooms: 4**
**Bathrooms: 2½**
**Width: 70' - 8"**
**Depth: 54' - 0"**
**Foundation: Crawlspace, Unfinished Basement**

**search online @ eplans.com**

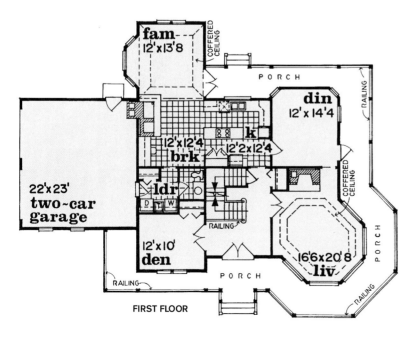

FIRST FLOOR

SECOND FLOOR

## plan # HPK1100040

**Style: FARMHOUSE**
First Floor: 1,362 sq. ft.
Second Floor: 1,270 sq. ft.
Total: 2,632 sq. ft.
Bedrooms: 4
Bathrooms: 2½
Width: 79' - 0"
Depth: 44' - 0"
Foundation: Unfinished
Basement, Crawlspace

**search online @ eplans.com**

**Rich with Victorian details**—scalloped shingles, a wraparound veranda, and turrets—this beautiful facade conceals a modern floor plan. Archways announce a distinctive tray-ceilinged living room and help define the dining room. An octagonal den across from the foyer provides a private spot for reading or studying. The U-shaped island kitchen holds an octagonal breakfast bay and a pass-through breakfast bar to the family room. Upstairs, three family bedrooms share a hall bath—one bedroom is within a turret. The master suite is complete with a sitting room with a bay window, along with a fancy bath set in another of the turrets.

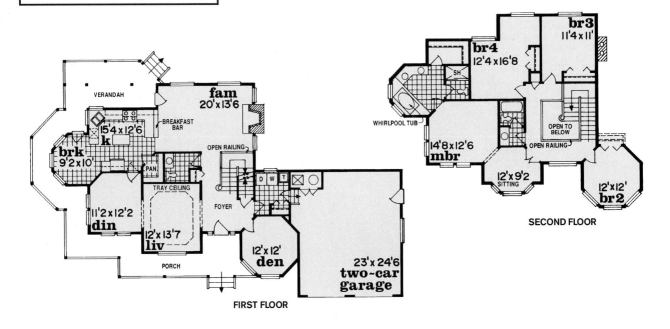

FIRST FLOOR

SECOND FLOOR

plan# HPK1100041

**Style: FARMHOUSE**
First Floor: 1,464 sq. ft.
Second Floor: 1,054 sq. ft.
Total: 2,518 sq. ft.
Bonus Space: 332 sq. ft.
Bedrooms: 4
Bathrooms: 3
Width: 59' - 0"
Depth: 51' - 6"
Foundation: Crawlspace

**search online @ eplans.com**

**Country Victoriana embellishes** this beautiful home. Perfect for a corner lot, this home begs for porch swings and lemonade. Inside, extra-high ceilings expand the space, as a thoughtful floor plan invites family and friends. The two-story great room enjoys a warming fireplace and wonderful rear views. The country kitchen has a preparation island and easily serves the sunny bayed nook and the formal dining room. To the far left, a bedroom serves as a perfect guest room; to the far right, a turret houses a private den. Upstairs, two bedrooms (one in a turret) share a full bath and ample bonus space. The master suite opens through French doors to reveal a grand bedroom and a sumptuous bath with a bumped-out spa tub.

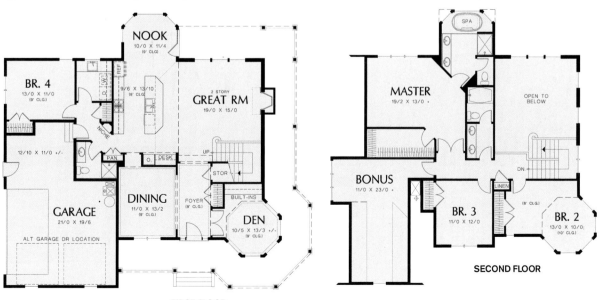

FIRST FLOOR

SECOND FLOOR

## plan# HPK1100042

**Style: PLANTATION**
First Floor: 2,578 sq. ft.
Second Floor: 1,277 sq. ft.
Total: 3,855 sq. ft.
Bedrooms: 4
Bathrooms: 4
Width: 53' - 6"
Depth: 97' - 0"
Foundation: Pier
(same as Piling)

search online @ eplans.com

**This charming Charleston design** is full of surprises! Perfect for a narrow footprint, the raised foundation is ideal for a waterfront location. An entry porch introduces a winding staircase. To the right is a living room/library that functions as a formal entertaining space. A large hearth and two sets of French doors to the covered porch enhance the great room. The master suite is positioned for privacy and includes great amenities that work to relax the homeowners. Upstairs, three family bedrooms, two full baths, an open media room, and a future game room create a fantastic casual family space.

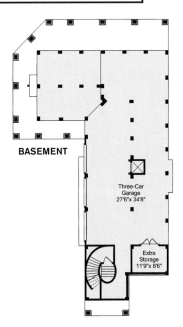

**BASEMENT**

Three-Car Garage
27'6"x 34'8"

Extra Storage
11'9"x 8'6"

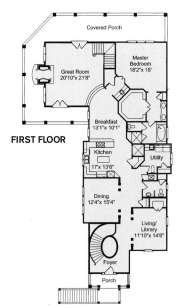

**FIRST FLOOR**

Covered Porch

Great Room
20'10"x 21'8"

Master Bedroom
18'2"x 16'

Breakfast
13'1"x 10'1"

Kitchen
17'x 13'6"

Utility

Dining
12'4"x 15'4"

Living/Library
11'10"x 14'6"

Foyer

Porch

**SECOND FLOOR**

Bedroom
17'10"x 11'1"

Media Room
8'7"x 21'

Bedroom
17'4"x 11'1"

Bedroom
13'2"x 11'4"

Future Gameroom
27'x 12'10"

**plan # HPK1100043**

Style: **FARMHOUSE**
First Floor: **3,566 sq. ft.**
Second Floor: **864 sq. ft.**
Total: **4,430 sq. ft.**
Bedrooms: **4**
Bathrooms: **4½**
Width: **127' - 9"**
Depth: **75' - 8"**
Foundation: **Finished Basement**

search online @ eplans.com

**Arch-topped windows, graceful details,** and a stunning stucco facade give this manor plenty of appeal. Inside, the foyer is flanked by a cozy drawing room and the formal dining room. Entertaining will be a breeze with the huge keeping room near the efficient kitchen, and the grand room; both rooms have fireplaces and access to the covered rear terrace. A guest suite provides privacy for visitors. The lavish master suite features a walk-in closet, deluxe bath, covered balcony, and fireplace. Upstairs, two amenity-filled suites are separated by a balcony. The basement level of the home expands its livability greatly, with a spacious exercise room (complete with a full bath), a summer kitchen, a gathering room (includes a fireplace and bar), and a suite for future needs. Note the studio apartment over the main garage.

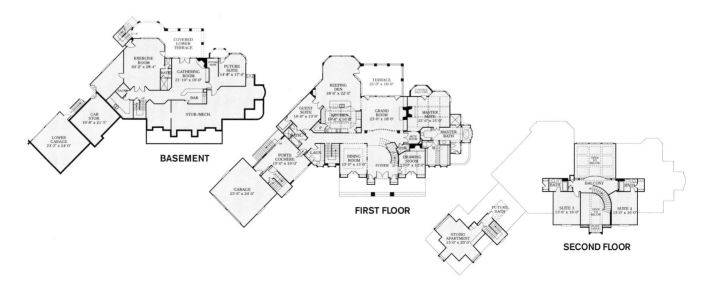

BASEMENT

FIRST FLOOR

SECOND FLOOR

**plan # HPK1100044**

**Style: FARMHOUSE**
First Floor: 2,151 sq. ft.
Second Floor: 738 sq. ft.
Total: 2,889 sq. ft.
Bonus Space: 534 sq. ft.
Bedrooms: 3
Bathrooms: 2½
Width: 99' - 0"
Depth: 56' - 0"
Foundation: Crawlspace

**search online @ eplans.com**

**A wide, welcoming porch and plenty** of stone accents highlight the facade of this charming symmetrical design. Inside, coffered ceilings enhance the study, great room, and breakfast nook; the dining room and master suite both boast stepped ceilings. From the great room, four sets of French doors open to a wrap-around rear porch with a grilling area. The master bedroom, also with porch access, includes built-in shelves, a walk-in closet with a window seat, and a luxurious bath with a whirlpool tub. On the second floor, two family bedrooms share a full bath with a whirlpool tub; a loft area and a bonus room offer extra space.

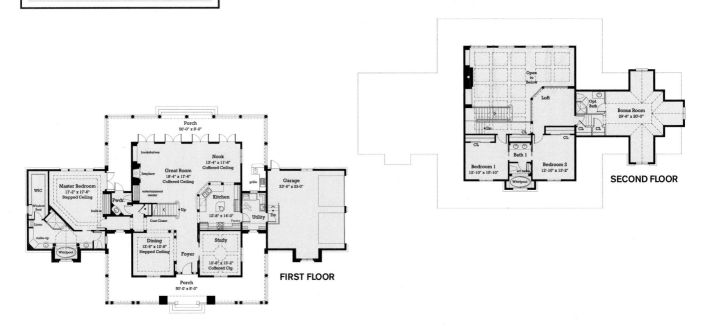

**plan # HPK1100045**

**Style: FARMHOUSE**
**Square Footage: 2,329**
**Bedrooms: 3**
**Bathrooms: 2½**
**Width: 72' - 6"**
**Depth: 73' - 4"**
**Foundation: Crawlspace**

search online @ eplans.com

**Stately columns and bright** windows grace the entry to this French farmhouse. Open rooms, French doors, and specialty ceilings add a sense of spaciousness throughout the home. Interior columns set the formal dining room apart. The great room boasts a fireplace, built-in cabinetry, and dazzling views. The master suite leads to His and Hers walk-in closets, a dual-sink vanity, a corner whirlpool tub, and an oversize corner shower. Two bedrooms with a shared bath sit in the right wing.

**Garage**
23'-0" x 21'-0"

opt. Stairs to garage attic storage/bonus room

**Porch**
12'-4" x 22'-0"

**Pwdr.**

**Utility**

**Nook**
10'-8" x 12'-0"

**Bedroom 2**
12'-0" x 12'-4"

**Master Suite**
14'-8" x 15'-0"
Tray Ceiling

built-in

**Great Room**
18'-10" x 17'-10"
Coffered Ceiling

fireplace

built-in

**Kitchen**
11'-2" x 12'-11"

P

**CL**

**Bath**

**Her WIC**

**His WIC**

**Dining**
11'-0" x 11'-4"
Coffered Ceiling

L

**Bench**

**Master Bath**

**Study**
11'-10" x 11'-0"
Beamed Ceiling

**Foyer**

**CL**

**Bedroom 1**
12'-0" x 11'-0"

**Porch**
12'-4" x 22'-0"

## plan # HPK1100046

**Style:** PLANTATION
**Square Footage:** 2,946
**Bedrooms:** 4
**Bathrooms:** 3
**Width:** 94' - 1"
**Depth:** 67' - 4"
**Foundation:** Slab

**search online @ eplans.com**

**This home's varying hipped-roof planes** make a strong statement. Exquisite classical detailing includes delightfully proportioned columns below a modified pedimented gable and masses of brick punctuated by corner quoins. The central foyer, with its high ceiling, leads to interesting traffic patterns. This extremely functional floor plan fosters flexible living patterns. There are formal and informal living areas, which are well defined by the living and family rooms. The sunken family room, wonderfully spacious with its high, sloping ceiling, contains a complete media-center wall and a fireplace flanked by doors to the entertainment patio. Occupying the isolated end of the floor plan, the master suite includes an adjacent office/den with a private porch.

**plan# HPK1100047**

**A covered porch and siding facade** add color and dimension to this delightful one-and-a-half story home. A convenient floor plan offers a favorable first impression. Turned stairs with rich wood finishes, a grand opening to the great room, fireplace wall as a focal point, and the introduction of natural light with the multiple windows combine to add spectacular design elements. A secondary hall offers convenient access to the kitchen and master suite. The large breakfast area and open kitchen with island create a delightful family work and gathering area. A first-floor master bedroom with raised ceiling, super bath, and walk-in closet create a luxurious retreat. The second-floor balcony offers a breathtaking view to the open foyer and leads to two additional bedrooms, a bath, and storage space.

**Style: FARMHOUSE**
First Floor: 1,263 sq. ft.
Second Floor: 434 sq. ft.
Total: 1,697 sq. ft.
Bedrooms: 3
Bathrooms: 2½
Width: 55' - 2"
Depth: 57' - 3"
Foundation: Unfinished Basement

search online @ eplans.com

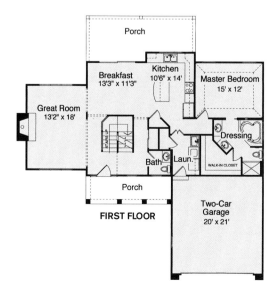

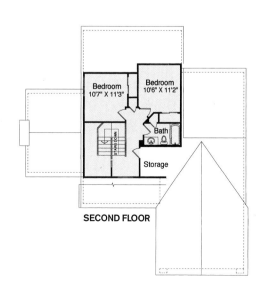

# Georgian and Federal Designs

**The symmetry of this facade, found on page 85, gives way to a kitchen-centric, modern interior.**

Georgian-style homes were popular throughout the American Colonies in the 18th Century. Imported from England like many ideas of the time, the style was identified with a long line of Kings named George, but actually was adopted from the Italian Renaissance. It caught on quickly in the Colonies, and was far-reaching; its popularity spread along the eastern seaboard, from what is now Maine to Georgia. The classical details of Georgian architecture gained a particularly strong foothold in the American South, which still endures today.

Balance and symmetry reign in Georgian design. Typically two stories, this style home is most easily identified by its elaborate entryway and central, paneled door, topped with a row of small windows or lined with sidelights. Above the front door is always a crown, supported on pilasters or flattened columns on either side of the door. Other defining features of the Georgian style include a cornice with decorative wood molding, multi-paned double hung windows, and hipped roofs.

Prevalent at the turn of the 19th Century, Federalist architecture is often seen as an American symbol of independence from British ways. It is in essence a rectangle with a central hall and the beginning of the four-square concept, with two rooms in the front and two in the back, off of a central hall. As with the Georgian, symmetry guides placement of windows and doors, but Federalist design is more gracefully proportioned, often with wings on either side. In the South, the federalist home was often detailed with curved or Palladian windows, and interiors were likely to have curved walls or ceiling treatments, with arched doorways and ornamental flourishes. ■

# Timeless Georgian

*Georgian style is identified by its generous proportions and rhythmic window patterns*

Georgian architecture is just as popular in the 21st Century as it was in Colonial times, and this luxurious Southern-style example makes it clear why. The exterior features of this outstanding design are pure Georgian, from classically rendered windows with distinct trim, to a pediment gable ornamented with cornice work and dentils, to perfectly proportioned columns that graciously mark the entrance.

**Above: Stately columns add an air of sophistication to this fine Georgian home.**
**Right: A twin curving staircase adorns the foyer.**

**Above:** A romantic fireplace warms the master bedroom French doors on either side of the fireplace lead to a private balcony. **Left:** The appealing design of the rear facade continues the ornament from the front.

Arriving through the portico to the front entry hall, visitors are greeted by a lavish, double-sided curved staircase. There is a natural flow for circulation, with living room and study to the right, leading to the great room in the rear. The dining room, kitchen with pantry, laundry room, and breakfast room are situated to the left. A generously proportioned terrace in the back makes the perfect outdoor gathering space.

Above the grand stair, a master bedroom suite opens to the balcony, and when the bedroom doors are open there are long views to the front yard. An extension over the garage allows for a room-size walk-in closet in the master bedroom, as well as a full bath in one of the family bedrooms. ■

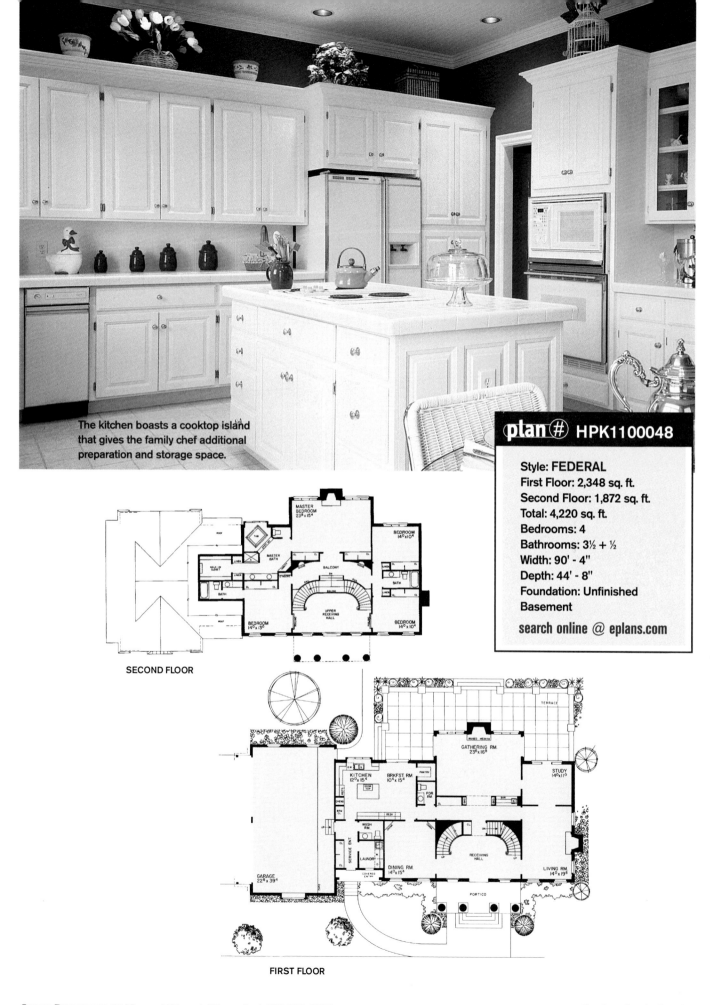

The kitchen boasts a cooktop island that gives the family chef additional preparation and storage space.

**plan# HPK1100048**

Style: FEDERAL
First Floor: 2,348 sq. ft.
Second Floor: 1,872 sq. ft.
Total: 4,220 sq. ft.
Bedrooms: 4
Bathrooms: 3½ + ½
Width: 90' - 4"
Depth: 44' - 8"
Foundation: Unfinished Basement

search online @ eplans.com

SECOND FLOOR

FIRST FLOOR

# Georgian & Federal Designs

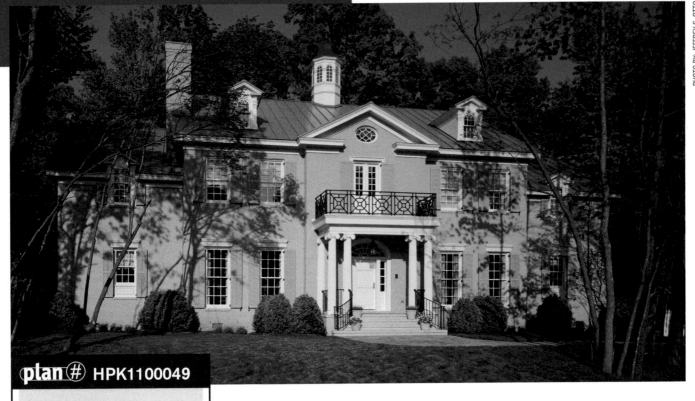

## plan # HPK1100049

**Style: GEORGIAN**
**First Floor:** 3,463 sq. ft.
**Second Floor:** 1,924 sq. ft.
**Total:** 5,387 sq. ft.
**Bedrooms:** 4
**Bathrooms:** 5½
**Width:** 88' - 6"
**Depth:** 98' - 0"
**Foundation:** Crawlspace, Basement

**search online @ eplans.com**

**This magnificent home** offers 4 bedrooms, 5½ baths, and curb appeal to beat the band. The elegant foyer opens to the library, the formal dining room, and the breathtaking living room. To the right, find the kitchen, breakfast nook, and the cozy keeping room. The master suite finds privacy on the far left. The second floor holds three additional bedrooms, four full baths and a rec room.

**FIRST FLOOR**

**SECOND FLOOR**

ORDER BLUEPRINTS 24 HOURS, 7 DAYS A WEEK, AT 1-800-521-6797

**plan # HPK1100050**

Style: **FEDERAL**
First Floor: 1,559 sq. ft.
Second Floor: 1,404 sq. ft.
Total: 2,963 sq. ft.
Bedrooms: 4
Bathrooms: 2½ + ½
Width: 66' - 10"
Depth: 44' - 10"
Foundation: Unfinished Basement

search online @ eplans.com

**Reminiscent of the stately character** of Federal architecture during an earlier period in our history, this two-story home is replete with exquisite detailing. The cornice work, pediment gable, dentils, brick corner quoins, beautifully proportioned columns, front-door detailing, window treatment, and massive twin chimneys are among the features that make this design so unique and appealing. Livability is great as well. Notice the quiet study, the beamed-ceiling family room, and the large formal living room. The four bedrooms are located upstairs.

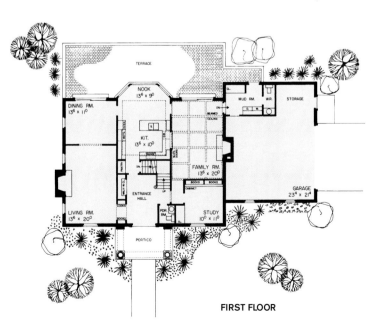

FIRST FLOOR

SECOND FLOOR

## plan# HPK1100051

**Style: FEDERAL**
First Floor: 3,505 sq. ft.
Second Floor: 1,302 sq. ft.
Total: 4,807 sq. ft.
Bedrooms: 5
Bathrooms: 4½
Width: 89' - 4"
Depth: 87' - 0"
Foundation: Slab

search online @ eplans.com

**This majestic Early American mansion** presents a sturdy, formal outside appearance; inside, it is especially well suited for a large family that likes big informal get-togethers. The huge family room, with a corner fireplace that merges with a dining nook and adjoins the country-style kitchen, will surely be the center of activity. Five bedrooms are placed throughout the home's two levels, including a glorious master suite with all the comforts you've ever dreamed about. A game room joins three bedrooms upstairs. For formal socializing, the dining area and living room are easily entered from the foyer, which guests reach through the impressive pillars of the covered entry. A den, or make it a study, is also located near the front. To the rear is a covered patio, perfect for meals alfresco.

FIRST FLOOR

SECOND FLOOR

**plan# HPK1100052**

**Style: FEDERAL**
**First Floor:** 2,139 sq. ft.
**Second Floor:** 2,147 sq. ft.
**Total:** 4,286 sq. ft.
**Bedrooms:** 4
**Bathrooms:** 3½ + ½
**Width:** 62' - 0"
**Depth:** 63' - 6"
**Foundation: Unfinished**
**Walkout Basement**

**search online @ eplans.com**

**The exterior of this home speaks volumes on** its appeal, but once inside, the distinctive layout has the last word. Traditionally formal spaces blend with a more modern, open design to increase the livability of the home. This is best exemplified with the flow from the grand room to the kitchen/breakfast nook, and into the family room. This functionality is ideal for family interaction or entertaining. The second floor houses the master suite, a grand retreat for the homeowners—adorned with a private sitting area, tray ceilings, and an expansive walk-in closet.

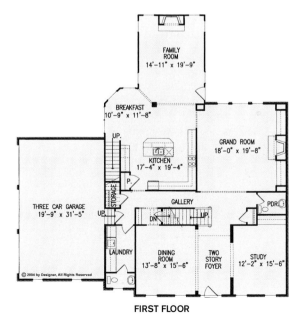

**FIRST FLOOR**

**SECOND FLOOR**

## plan# HPK1100053

**LD**

Style: **GEORGIAN**
First Floor: 2,126 sq. ft.
Second Floor: 1,882 sq. ft.
Total: 4,008 sq. ft.
Bedrooms: 4
Bathrooms: 2½
Width: 92' - 0"
Depth: 64' - 4"
Foundation: Unfinished
Basement

**search online @ eplans.com**

**This historical Georgian home has its roots** in the 18th Century. The full two-story center section is delightfully complemented by the one-and-a-half-story wings. An elegant gathering room, three steps down from the rest of the house, provides ample space for entertaining on a grand scale. The study and the formal dining room flank the foyer. Each of these rooms has a fireplace as its highlight. The breakfast room, kitchen, powder room, and laundry room are arranged for maximum efficiency. The second floor houses the family bedrooms. Take special note of the spacious master suite.

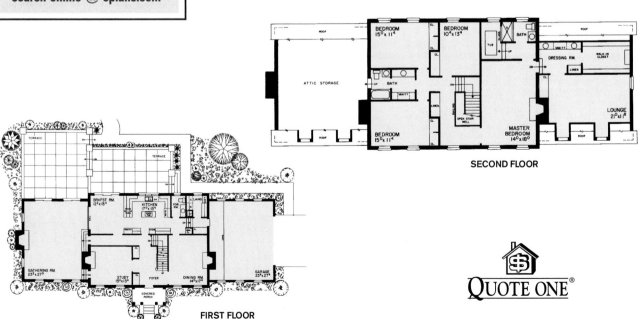

**SECOND FLOOR**

**FIRST FLOOR**

QUOTE ONE®

**plan# HPK1100054**

Style: **FEDERAL**
First Floor: 2,187 sq. ft.
Second Floor: 1,118 sq. ft.
Total: 3,305 sq. ft.
Bonus Space: 328 sq. ft.
Bedrooms: 4
Bathrooms: 3½
Width: 81' - 2"
Depth: 41' - 2"
Foundation: Crawlspace

search online @ eplans.com

**The essence of Early America is captured** in this timeless Federal design. The expansive family room is adorned with a vaulted ceiling and fireplace. The adjacent master suite features His and Hers vanities and a large wardrobe. Upstairs, a balcony provides an overhead view of the family room and foyer. Three additional family bedrooms share two full baths. Laundry rooms on both floors is an added bonus.

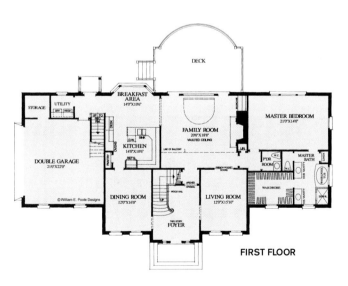

**FIRST FLOOR**

**SECOND FLOOR**

© William E. Poole Designs, Inc.

## plan# HPK1100055

Style: **GEORGIAN**
First Floor: 2,798 sq. ft.
Second Floor: 1,496 sq. ft.
Total: 4,294 sq. ft.
Bonus Space: 515 sq. ft.
Bedrooms: 4
Bathrooms: 3½
Width: 91' - 10"
Depth: 57' - 2"
Foundation: Crawlspace,
Unfinished Basement
**search online @ eplans.com**

**This classic Georgian design captures** old-world charm with modern amenities. A spacious library boasts a built-in bookcase and central fireplace. A second fireplace warms the family room, large island kitchen, and breakfast area. Convenient access to the rear porch makes outdoor dining an option. A private elevator takes luxury to new heights. Once upstairs, bedroom #2—enhanced by a personal fireplace—is outfitted with a built-in bookcase, a huge wardrobe, a spacious storage area, and a full bath with whirlpool tub. Two additional family bedrooms share a full bath. An expansive rec room completes this level. Extra storage space in the garage is an addded bonus.

**FIRST FLOOR**

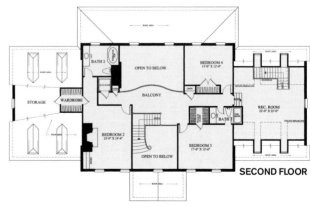

**SECOND FLOOR**

© William E. Poole Designs, Inc.

## plan# HPK1100056

**Style: GEORGIAN**
First Floor: 3,027 sq. ft.
Second Floor: 1,509 sq. ft.
Total: 4,536 sq. ft.
Bedrooms: 5
Bathrooms: 4½
Width: 85' - 0"
Depth: 82' - 6"
Foundation: Crawlspace,
Unfinished Basement

**search online @ eplans.com**

**This home retains an elegant air** while presenting a gracious and welcoming facade. Inside find plenty of space for both formal and casual events. A dining room and hearth-warmed living room flank the foyer, and a library is tucked in back to the right. The family room enjoys a fireplace and great views of the outdoors, as well as open flow into the breakfast area and kitchen. A large utility room expands the kitchen's space to the front of the plan. The master suite on the right is made extra-special by its deluxe bath. Plenty of dressing space is surrounded by an enormous double wardrobe, double vanities, a compartmented toilet, and a stunning whirlpool tub set in a curved bay window. Four more bedrooms reside on the second floor, each with its own bath and plenty of closet space. Two handy storage spaces flank the bedrooms, and a wealth of unfinished attic storage awaits above the garage.

**FIRST FLOOR**

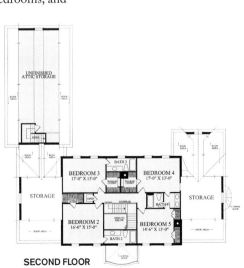

**SECOND FLOOR**

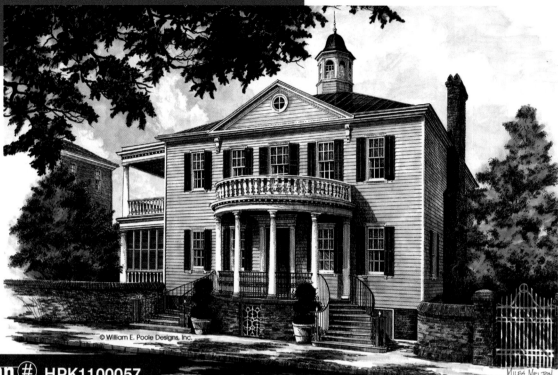

© William E. Poole Designs, Inc.

MILES MELTON
CARY, NC

## plan # HPK1100057

**Style: GEORGIAN**
First Floor: 2,064 sq. ft.
Second Floor: 1,521 sq. ft.
Total: 3,585 sq. ft.
Bonus Space: 427 sq. ft.
Bedrooms: 4
Bathrooms: 3
Width: 84' - 8"
Depth: 65' - 0"
Foundation: Crawlspace

**search online @ eplans.com**

**The best of Southern tradition combines** with an easygoing floor plan to make this home a sure neighborhood favorite. The elegant portico at the front is a unique touch. Formal rooms—a library, living room and dining room—surround the two-story foyer, which leads past the staircase to the hearth-warmed family room. In the very back, the kitchen is amplified by a gorgeous vaulted sunroom, featuring two walls of windows to let in light. The second floor is home to a deluxe master suite, as well as two family bedrooms that share a bath. A utility room is conveniently located upstairs as well. Future space is available for expansion over the garage.

**FIRST FLOOR**

**SECOND FLOOR**

plan# HPK1100058

**A grand facade detailed with brick corner quoins,** stucco flourishes, arched windows, and an elegant entrance presents this home. A spacious foyer is accented by curving stairs and flanked by a formal living room and a formal dining room. For cozy times, a through-fireplace is located between a large family room and a quiet study. The master bedroom is designed to pamper, with two walk-in closets, a two-sided fireplace, a bayed sitting area, and a lavish private bath. Upstairs, three secondary bedrooms each have a private bath and a walk-in closet. Also on this level is a spacious recreation room, perfect for a game room or children's playroom.

Style: GEORGIAN
First Floor: 3,599 sq. ft.
Second Floor: 1,621 sq. ft.
Total: 5,220 sq. ft.
Bonus Space: 537 sq. ft.
Bedrooms: 4
Bathrooms: 5½
Width: 108' - 10"
Depth: 53' - 10"
Foundation: Slab, Unfinished Basement

search online @ eplans.com

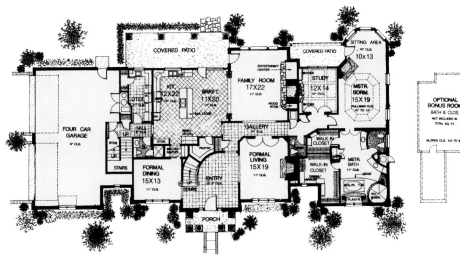

**FIRST FLOOR**

**SECOND FLOOR**

**plan# HPK1100059**

Style: **FEDERAL**
First Floor: 2,432 sq. ft.
Second Floor: 903 sq. ft.
Total: 3,335 sq. ft.
Bedrooms: 4
Bathrooms: 3½
Width: 90' - 0"
Depth: 53' - 10"
Foundation: Crawlspace, Slab,
Unfinished Basement

**search online @ eplans.com**

**The elegant symmetry of this four-bedroom** Southern traditional plan makes it a joy to own. Six columns frame the covered porch, and two chimneys add interest to the exterior roofline. The two-story foyer opens to the right to a formal living room with a built-in wet bar and a fireplace. A massive family room with a cathedral ceiling leads outside to a large covered patio or to the breakfast room and kitchen. A side-entry, three-car garage provides room for a golf cart and separate workshop area. The first-floor master bedroom features vaulted ceilings, a secluded covered patio, and a plant ledge in the master bath. The three bedrooms upstairs share two baths.

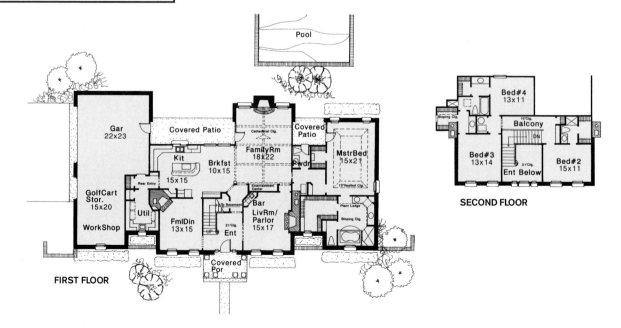

**plan# HPK1100060**

The charm of the Old South is designed into this stately Federal manor. A round entry portico leads to the two-story foyer with a circular staircase. The formal living room, dining room, and family room each feature distinctive fireplaces; the latter is also highlighted by a built-in entertainment center, walk-in wet bar, beamed cathedral ceiling, and access to a rear covered patio. Impressive 10-foot ceilings grace the entire first floor. The secluded master bedroom has a vaulted ceiling, three walk-in closets, and porch access. Four additional bedrooms on the second floor share adjoining baths.

**Style: FEDERAL**
First Floor: 3,294 sq. ft.
Second Floor: 1,300 sq. ft.
Total: 4,594 sq. ft.
Bedrooms: 5
Bathrooms: 3½
Width: 106' - 10"
Depth: 52' - 10"
Foundation: Unfinished Basement

search online @ eplans.com

SECOND FLOOR

FIRST FLOOR

## plan # HPK1100061

Style: Federal
Main Level: 2,419 sq. ft.
Upper Level: 1,519 sq. ft.
Lower Level: 1,243 sq. ft.
Total: 5,181 sq. ft.
Bedrooms: 6
Bathrooms: 4½
Width: 73' - 0"
Depth: 61' - 0"
Foundation: Finished Walkout Basement

search online @ eplans.com

**A vintage look dating back** to Early America gives this home undeniable curb appeal. Inside, a two-story entry welcomes visitors. Beyond the curving staircase sits the master suite. The adjacent study is a calculated detail aimed to please the homeowner. A see-through fireplace adds ambiance and warmth to the living room and adjoining breakfast nook. Sliding glass doors lead from the family room to the vaulted 3 seasons room. The rear deck extends the living space outdoors. The spacious laundry room acts as a mud room, with built-in lockers, a built-in seat, and room to remove shoes and coats. The second floor houses four additional bedrooms, one pair separated by a Jack-and-Jill bath, and the second pair sharing a full hall bath. A laundry chute in the hall bath is an added convenience. A gameroom completes this level.

LOWER LEVEL

MAIN LEVEL

UPPER LEVEL

**The classic styling of this brick American** traditional home will be respected for years to come. The formidable, double-door, transomed entry and a Palladian window reveal the shining foyer within. The spacious dining room and the formal study or living room flank the foyer; a large family room with a full wall of glass conveniently opens to the breakfast room and the kitchen. The master suite features a spacious sitting area with its own fireplace and a tray ceiling. Two additional bedrooms share a bath, and a fourth bedroom has its own private bath.

**plan# HPK1100062**

Style: **GEORGIAN**
First Floor: **1,554 sq. ft.**
Second Floor: **1,648 sq. ft.**
Total: **3,202 sq. ft.**
Bedrooms: **4**
Bathrooms: **3½**
Width: **60' - 0"**
Depth: **43' - 0"**
Foundation: **Walkout Basement**

search online @ eplans.com

QUOTE ONE®

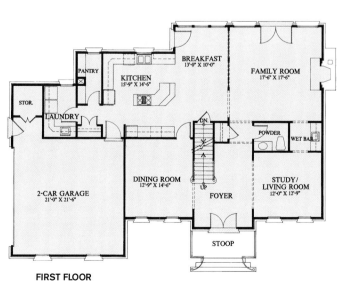

**FIRST FLOOR**

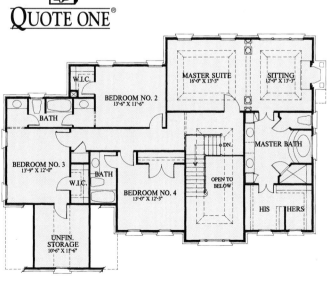

**SECOND FLOOR**

© William E. Poole Designs, Inc.

## plan # HPK1100063

**Style: FEDERAL**
**First Floor:** 2,492 sq. ft.
**Second Floor:** 1,313 sq. ft.
**Total:** 3,805 sq. ft.
**Bonus Space:** 687 sq. ft.
**Bedrooms:** 4
**Bathrooms:** 3½ + ½
**Width:** 85' - 10"
**Depth:** 54' - 6"
**Foundation:** Crawlspace,
**Unfinished Basement**

**search online @ eplans.com**

**Although the exterior of this Georgian home** is entirely classical, the interior boasts an up-to-date floor plan that's a perfect fit for today's lifestyles. The large central family room, conveniently near the kitchen and breakfast area, includes a fireplace and access to the rear terrace; fireplaces also grace the formal dining room and library. The master suite, also with terrace access, features a spacious walk-in closet and a bath with a whirlpool tub. Upstairs, a second master suite—great for guests—joins two family bedrooms. Nearby, a large open area can serve as a recreation room.

**SECOND FLOOR**

**FIRST FLOOR**

**An elegant front entrance welcomes you** to this classically styled home. Inside, a hall leads past the living room (or study) and formal dining room to the spacious family room. You may wish to stop here and enjoy the fireplace, or use the French doors to go out onto the rear covered porch. An island kitchen is convenient to both the dining room and a sunny breakfast room. Guests will be grateful for the privacy of the guest bedroom, located behind the two-car garage and offering access to the porch. The family sleeping zone is upstairs and includes a master suite with fireplace and deluxe bath plus two secondary bedrooms and an unfinished open space for future expansion.

**plan# HPK1100064**

Style: **FEDERAL**
First Floor: 1,959 sq. ft.
Second Floor: 1,408 sq. ft.
Total: 3,367 sq. ft.
Bedrooms: 4
Bathrooms: 3½
Width: 61' - 9"
Depth: 62' - 9"
Foundation: Walkout Basement

**search online @ eplans.com**

## plan # HPK1100065

Style: **FEDERAL**
First Floor: 900 sq. ft.
Second Floor: 870 sq. ft.
Total: 1,770 sq. ft.
Bonus Space: 198 sq. ft.
Bedrooms: 3
Bathrooms: 2½
Width: 45' - 0"
Depth: 36' - 11"
Foundation: Unfinished Basement

**search online @ eplans.com**

**A pediment gable, echoed over the entry** and the garage, and pilastered corners reveal the Georgian heritage of this design. Inside, columned arches mark the boundaries of the massive great room, where a triple window overlooks the rear deck and the kitchen and breakfast rooms. The second floor offers three bedrooms, including a master suite with a deluxe bath. Two family bedrooms share a full bath and adjoin a spacious bonus room.

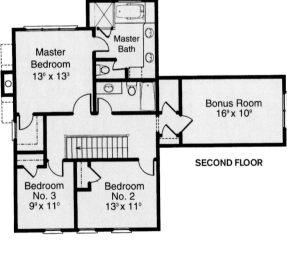

SECOND FLOOR

FIRST FLOOR

© William E. Poole Designs, Inc.

**Fine living is guaranteed** in this stately Early American home. The front living and dining rooms are laid out side-by-side for gracious entertaining, and service from the huge country-style kitchen will be convenient and smooth. To the left of the kitchen, the ceiling in the great room soars two stories above the hearth-warmed room. The first-floor master suite with a sumptuous bath is considerately separated from the three family bedrooms located upstairs. Also on the second floor is space for a future recreation room.

**plan# HPK1100066**

Style: **GEORGIAN**
First Floor: 1,816 sq. ft.
Second Floor: 968 sq. ft.
Total: 2,784 sq. ft.
Bonus Space: 402 sq. ft.
Bedrooms: 4
Bathrooms: 3½
Width: 54' - 6"
Depth: 52' - 8"
Foundation: Crawlspace

**search online @ eplans.com**

**FIRST FLOOR**

**SECOND FLOOR**

© William E. Poole Designs, Inc.

## plan# HPK1100067

**Style: GEORGIAN**
First Floor: 2,273 sq. ft.
Second Floor: 1,391 sq. ft.
Total: 3,664 sq. ft.
Bonus Space: 547 sq. ft.
Bedrooms: 4
Bathrooms: 4½
Width: 77' - 2"
Depth: 48' - 0"
Foundation: Crawlspace

**search online @ eplans.com**

**An easy and charming interpretation** of the Late Georgian style, this plan is carefully adapted to meet the practical requirements of a modern lifestyle. Cased openings, high ceilings, and well-placed windows keep the expansive, comfortable interiors well-lighted and open. The spacious family room, which enjoys a fireplace flanked by built-in shelves, opens to the rear terrace. The lavish master suite enjoys privacy on the first level; the other three bedrooms—each with private baths—are comfortably situated on the second floor. Additional space is available upstairs to develop a recreation room.

**FIRST FLOOR**

© William E. Poole Designs

**SECOND FLOOR**

# Georgian & Federal Designs

**This grand two-story home proves** that tried-and-true traditional style is still the best! Thoughtful planning brings formal living areas to the forefront and places open, casual living areas to the rear of the plan. Bedroom 4 serves as a multipurpose room, providing the flexibility desired by today's homeowner. The second floor is devoted to the relaxing master suite, two secondary bedrooms, a full hall bath, and a balcony overlook.

Style: **GEORGIAN**
First Floor: 1,135 sq. ft.
Second Floor: 917 sq. ft.
Total: 2,052 sq. ft.
Bonus Space: 216 sq. ft.
Bedrooms: 4
Bathrooms: 3
Width: 52' - 4"
Depth: 37' - 6"
Foundation: Slab, Crawlspace, Unfinished Walkout Basement

search online @ eplans.com

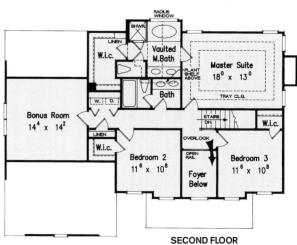

FIRST FLOOR

SECOND FLOOR

# Georgian & Federal Designs

## plan # HPK1100069

**Style: GEORGIAN**
First Floor: 1,679 sq. ft.
Second Floor: 1,605 sq. ft.
Total: 3,284 sq. ft.
Bedrooms: 5
Bathrooms: 4
Width: 57' - 0"
Depth: 45' - 4"
Foundation: Crawlspace,
Unfinished Walkout Basement

**search online @ eplans.com**

**This stately Georgian home combines** varied rooflines, a grand pediment entry, and eye-catching brick to create a place your family will delight in for generations. Inside, an intriguing floor plan directs traffic for increased flow and maximizes natural light. The foyer opens on the right to a formal dining room with a box-bay window and reveals a study on the left. An expansive kitchen features an island and a serving bar that views the bayed breakfast nook. Stunning vistas grace the two-story family room, courtesy of a rear bowed window wall. A see-through fireplace is shared with the sun room. Three upstairs bedrooms are generously appointed. The master suite is a romantic retreat with a bayed sitting area and sumptuous bath with a window seat.

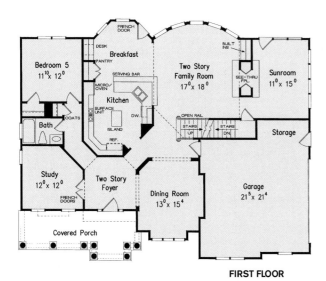

**FIRST FLOOR**

**SECOND FLOOR**

# Georgian & Federal Designs

plan# **HPK1100070**

**Style: FEDERAL**
**First Floor: 2,950 sq. ft.**
**Second Floor: 1,138 sq. ft.**
**Total: 4,088 sq. ft.**
**Bedrooms: 4**
**Bathrooms: 3½**
**Width: 77' - 0"**
**Depth: 56' - 0"**
**Foundation: Unfinished Basement**

search online @ eplans.com

**Steeped in Early American flair,** this four-bedroom home impresses from the first glance. Inside, the master suite occupies the entire left side of the first floor. To the right, the gourmet kitchen is nestled between the warmth emanating from fireplaces in both the grand and keeping rooms. Upstairs, bedroom 2 annexes a private, full bath. Bedrooms 3 and 4 share a Jack-and-Jill bath. The loft area is ideal for a family computer. A double garage and a separate single garage complete this plan.

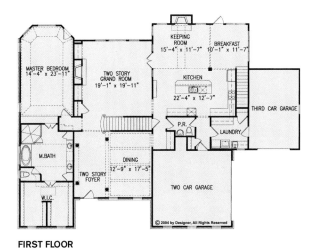

**FIRST FLOOR**

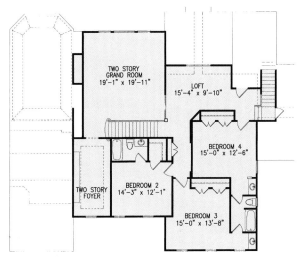

**SECOND FLOOR**

© William E. Poole Designs, Inc.

## plan⊕ HPK1100071

**Style: GEORGIAN**
First Floor: 2,168 sq. ft.
Second Floor: 1,203 sq. ft.
Total: 3,371 sq. ft.
Bonus Space: 452 sq. ft.
Bedrooms: 4
Bathrooms: 4½
Width: 71' - 2"
Depth: 63' - 4"
Foundation: Crawlspace,
Unfinished Basement

**search online @ eplans.com**

**This stately two-story beauty offers** the utmost in style and livability. The grand columned entryway is topped by a railed roof, making it the centerpiece of the facade. Formal space resides at the front of the plan, with a living room and dining room flanking the foyer. Secluded behind the staircase is the elegant master suite, with a huge walk-in closet and swanky private bath. The hearth-warmed family room flows into the island kitchen and breakfast nook, making this space the comfortable hub of home life. A laundry room and half-bath are convenient to this area. Upstairs, three bedrooms all have access to separate baths and share space with a future recreation room.

**FIRST FLOOR**

**SECOND FLOOR**

© William E. Poole Designs, Inc.

**This fine example of the Georgian style** of architecture offers a wonderful facade with Southern charm. The foyer is flanked by the formal dining room and the living room. The efficient kitchen is situated between the sunny breakfast nook and the dining room. The family room opens to the backyard. The master suite enjoys an opulent bath and large walk-in closet. The second floor presents three bedrooms and two baths.

**plan # HPK1100072**

Style: **GEORGIAN**
First Floor: 2,603 sq. ft.
Second Floor: 1,660 sq. ft.
Total: 4,263 sq. ft.
Bonus Space: 669 sq. ft.
Bedrooms: 4
Bathrooms: 4½ + ½
Width: 98' - 0"
Depth: 56' - 8"
Foundation: Unfinished Basement

search online @ eplans.com

**FIRST FLOOR**

**SECOND FLOOR**

© Stephen Fuller, Inc.

## plan# HPK1100073

**Style: GEORGIAN**
First Floor: 1,650 sq. ft.
Second Floor: 1,060 sq. ft.
Total: 2,710 sq. ft.
Bedrooms: 4
Bathrooms: 3½
Width: 53' - 0"
Depth: 68' - 2"
Foundation: Walkout
Basement

search online @ eplans.com

**This home features keystone arches** that frame the arched front door and windows. Inside, the foyer opens directly to the large great room with a fireplace and French doors that lead outside. Just off the foyer, the dining room is defined by columns. Adjacent to the breakfast room is the keeping room, which includes a corner fireplace and more French doors to the large rear porch. The master suite has dual vanities and a spacious walk-in closet. Upstairs, two family bedrooms enjoy separate access to a shared bath; down the hall, a fourth bedroom includes a private bath.

**FIRST FLOOR**

**SECOND FLOOR**

## plan# HPK1100074

**Style: FEDERAL**
First Floor: 1,536 sq. ft.
Second Floor: 679 sq. ft.
Total: 2,215 sq. ft.
Bedrooms: 3
Bathrooms: 2½
Width: 53' - 0"
Depth: 44' - 0"
Foundation: Unfinished Basement

search online @ eplans.com

**There is more to this Early American home than** a warm, inviting exterior. Inside, fireplaces warm each of the first-floor rooms—living room, country kitchen, and master bedroom. To the right of the foyer is the private master suite enhanced by a walk-in closet and a pampering bath that includes a soothing whirlpool tub, twin vanities, and a bath seat. To the rear of the plan, an L-shaped food preparation area conveniently connects via an island snack bar to a large country kitchen perfect for informal gatherings. The formal living room and the laundry room complete this level. The second floor holds two secondary bedrooms, a full bath, and a lounge/study with a built-in desk.

**FIRST FLOOR**

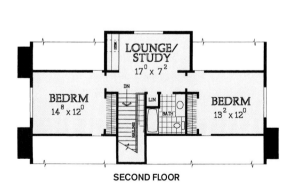

**SECOND FLOOR**

# Georgian & Federal Designs

© William E. Poole Designs, Inc.

## plan# HPK1100075

**Style: GEORGIAN**
Square Footage: 3,600
Bedrooms: 4
Bathrooms: 3½
Width: 76' - 2"
Depth: 100' - 10"
Foundation: Crawlspace,
Unfinished Basement

**search online @ eplans.com**

**Graceful columns combine** with stunning symmetry on this fine four-bedroom home. Inside, the foyer opens to the formal living room on the left and then leads back to the spacious family room. Here, a fireplace waits to warm cool fall evenings and built-ins accommodate your book collection. The efficient island kitchen offers plenty of counter and cabinet space, easily serving both the formal dining room and the sunny breakfast area. A separate bedroom resides back by the garage and features a walk-in closet. Two more family bedrooms are at the front right side of the home and share a full bath. The lavish master suite is complete with a huge walk-in closet, a bayed sitting area, and a sumptuous bath.

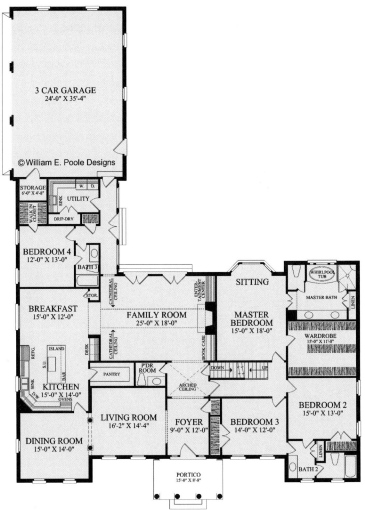

**plan# HPK1100076**

**This Early American recreation** is representative of the stately Federal styles of Colonial times. A beautifully curved stairway spirals into the foyer. To the left, double doors open to a family room. To the right, another set of double doors opens to a formal dining room. Straight ahead, the living room is brightened by a wall of windows overlooking the rear porch and is warmed by a cozy family fireplace. An island kitchen with a breakfast bar and a nook are located nearby. The garage conveniently connects directly to the kitchen. The first-floor master suite features rear-porch access, a private bath, and an enormous walk-in closet. Upstairs, four additional family bedrooms share two hall baths.

Style: **FEDERAL**
First Floor: 2,502 sq. ft.
Second Floor: 1,645 sq. ft.
Total: 4,147 sq. ft.
Bedrooms: 5
Bathrooms: 3½
Width: 95' - 0"
Depth: 51' - 0"
Foundation: Unfinished Basement

search online @ eplans.com

FIRST FLOOR

SECOND FLOOR

**plan# HPK1100077**

**Style: FEDERAL**
**First Floor:** 2,558 sq. ft.
**Second Floor:** 884 sq. ft.
**Total:** 3,442 sq. ft.
**Bedrooms:** 4
**Bathrooms:** 3½
**Width:** 73' - 1"
**Depth:** 64' - 3"
**Foundation:** Unfinished
**Walkout Basement**

**search online @ eplans.com**

Bold columns add a stately appeal to the Early American stylings of this two-story home. The covered porch gives way to the two-story foyer, flanked by a dining room—adorned with columns—and a vaulted study. The gallery leads to the lavish master suite, enhanced by a tray ceiling. A fireplace in the grand room faces the spacious, gourmet kitchen. A second fireplace in the keeping room will make it a family favorite. Upstairs, bedroom 2—complete with a private, full bath—is an ideal guest suite. Bedrooms 3 and 4 share a Jack-and-Jill bath. The large bonus room is a possible recreation room.

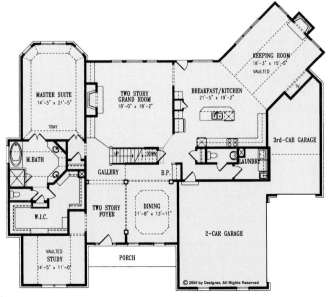

**FIRST FLOOR**

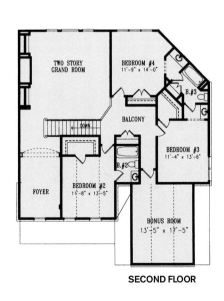

**SECOND FLOOR**

**The double wings, twin chimneys,** and center portico of this home work in concert to create a classic architectural statement. The two-story foyer is flanked by the spacious dining room and formal living room, each containing their own fireplaces. A large family room with a full wall of glass opens conveniently to the kitchen and breakfast room. The master suite features a tray ceiling and French doors that open to a covered porch. A grand master bath completes the master suite. Two family bedrooms share a bath, and another has a private bath. Bedroom 4 features a nook for sitting or reading.

**QUOTE ONE®**

**plan# HPK1100078**

**Style: GEORGIAN**
**First Floor:** 1,455 sq. ft.
**Second Floor:** 1,649 sq. ft.
**Total:** 3,104 sq. ft.
**Bedrooms:** 4
**Bathrooms:** 3½
**Width:** 54' - 4"
**Depth:** 46' - 0"
**Foundation:** Walkout Basement

**search online @ eplans.com**

FIRST FLOOR

COVERED PORCH

BREAKFAST
13'-2" x 10'-0"

TWO-CAR GARAGE
22'-0" x 21'-6"

FAMILY ROOM
15'-6" x 16'-0"

KITCHEN
13'-2" x 12'-0"

LAUNDRY
7'-10" x 7'-6"

LIVING ROOM
13'-6" x 12'-0"

TWO-STORY FOYER
15'-4" x 9'-2"

DINING ROOM
13'-4" x 15'-0"

SECOND FLOOR

COVERED PORCH

SITTING
9'-0" x 4'-8"

MASTER BATH
13'-4" x 15'-10"

BEDROOM No.4
16'-10" x 11'-10"

MASTER BEDROOM
15'-6" x 16'-0"

MASTER CLOSET

BATH

BATH

BEDROOM No.2
13'-4" x 12'-0"

OPEN TO FOYER BELOW

BEDROOM No.3
13'-4" x 12'-0"

# Georgian & Federal Designs

## plan # HPK1100079

**Style: GEORGIAN**
First Floor: 2,081 sq. ft.
Second Floor: 940 sq. ft.
Total: 3,021 sq. ft.
Bedrooms: 4
Bathrooms: 3½
Width: 69' - 9"
Depth: 65' - 0"
Foundation: Walkout
Basement

**search online @ eplans.com**

**This Georgian country-style home** displays an impressive appearance. The front porch and columns frame the elegant elliptical entrance. Georgian symmetry balances the living room and dining room off the foyer. The first floor continues into the two-story great room, which offers built-in cabinetry, a fireplace, and a large bay window that overlooks the rear deck. A dramatic tray ceiling, a wall of glass, and access to the rear deck complete the master bedroom. To the left of the great room, a large kitchen opens to a breakfast area with walls of windows. Upstairs, each of three family bedrooms features ample closet space as well as direct access to a bathroom.

FIRST FLOOR

SECOND FLOOR

# Greek Revival Homes

Wealthy Colonists settled in the South, attracted by its great agricultural potential and their affluence was often reflected in the homes they built. Greek Revival architecture, modeled on ancient Greek temples, dominated among the Southern homes built during the first half of the 19th Century.

Full-height classical columns supporting a portico are the hallmark of Greek Revivals. A simpler rendition of this feature includes pilasters applied along the front wall to visually support an entry porch roof. These homes are typically grand and symmetrical, with central entrances in front and back. Balconies, columns, and pillars are favored details.

Often there is a gable end facing the street. Inside, this style can be easily identified by its floor-length windows that allow cross ventilation and are perfectly suited to a Southern climate. Considered to be the very definition of Antebellum style, Greek Revival homes are noted for their spacious interiors, high ceilings, and sweeping staircases and they remain an integral part of Southern culture. ■

**Full-height columns are a defining element of the Greek Revival style, such as those on this home, found on page 123.**

# A Sense of Place

*This is the grand dame of antebellum Southern architecture*

Stately Greek Revival homes are often considered historical treasures that exemplify the architecture of the antebellum Southern states. This manor house has all the same grandeur of the past, with a floor plan designed for a contemporary lifestyle. And the hilltop setting here adds open vistas to the mix.

**Above: This new home looks at first like it has been part of the landscape for decades. Right: A wall of windows illuminates the family room, which is accented by a fireplace and columns.**

The upstairs hallway provides tremendous views, both down to the foyer and outside through the second-floor porch. Opposite: A fireplace lends warmth and charm to the formal dining room.

Symmetry reigns in this perfect rendition of Greek Revival architecture. The central portion of the home is based on the guiding principles of the four by four plan, with the addition of lower wings flanking each side to provide more space. This style of architecture defined the very concept of a portico, and it is rendered exquisitely in this home, with pediments and columns that provide a centerpiece to the classically symmetrical facade.

The plan is quite formal in the front, with a living room and dining room flanking the grand foyer, but more relaxed in the back, where a two-story gallery hall opens to a large family room with a great hearth, visually separated by the columns so typical of Southern-style architecture. More columns identify the breakfast area and island kitchen to the side. On the other side of the home is a master bedroom retreat, with a luxurious bath. Each of the three family bedrooms upstairs has a private bath. Also upstairs are an exercise room, recreation room, and office. ∎

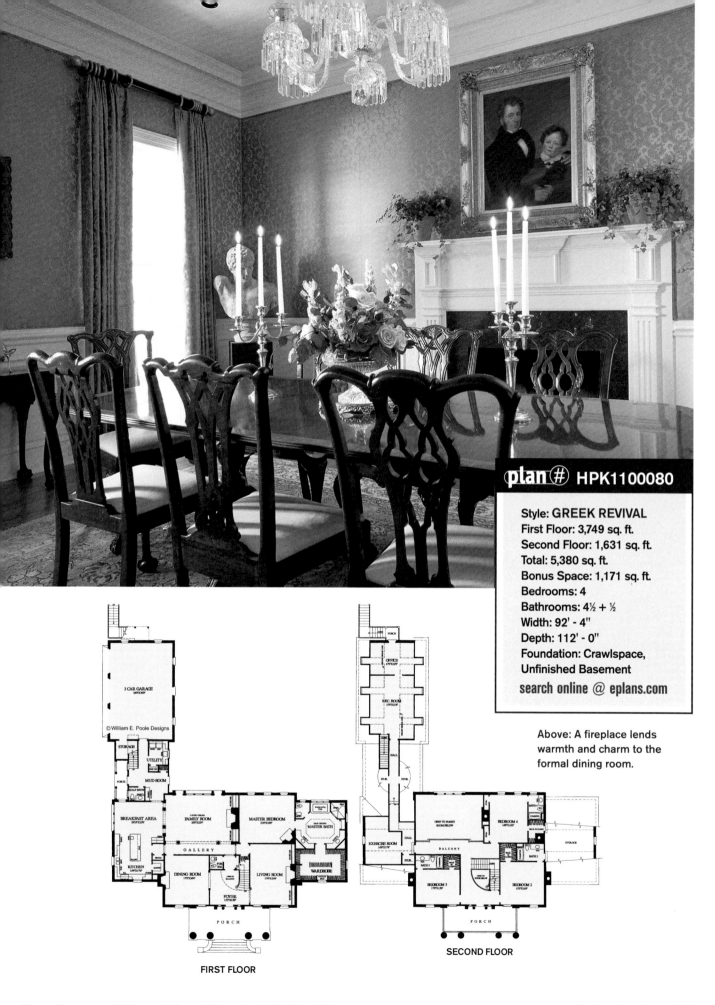

**plan# HPK1100080**

Style: **GREEK REVIVAL**
First Floor: 3,749 sq. ft.
Second Floor: 1,631 sq. ft.
Total: 5,380 sq. ft.
Bonus Space: 1,171 sq. ft.
Bedrooms: 4
Bathrooms: 4½ + ½
Width: 92' - 4"
Depth: 112' - 0"
Foundation: Crawlspace,
Unfinished Basement

**search online @ eplans.com**

**Above:** A fireplace lends warmth and charm to the formal dining room.

**FIRST FLOOR**

© William E. Poole Designs

3 CAR GARAGE

STORAGE
UTILITY
PORCH
MUD ROOM
HALF BATH

BREAKFAST AREA
FAMILY ROOM
MASTER BEDROOM
MASTER BATH

KITCHEN
GALLERY

DINING ROOM
LIVING ROOM
WARDROBE
FOYER

PORCH

**SECOND FLOOR**

PORCH

OFFICE

REC. ROOM

HALL
STOR.

EXERCISE ROOM
HALL
STOR.

OPEN TO FAMILY ROOM BELOW
BEDROOM 4

BALCONY
STORAGE

BATH 3
BATH 2

BEDROOM 3
OPEN TO FOYER BELOW
BEDROOM 2

PORCH

# Greek Revival Homes

© William E. Poole Designs, Inc.

## plan # HPK1100081

**Style: GREEK REVIVAL**
Main Level: 4,556 sq. ft.
Upper Level: 3,261 sq. ft.
Lower Level: 2,918 sq. ft.
Total: 10,735 sq. ft.
Bedrooms: 6
Bathrooms: 7½ + ½
Width: 97' - 2"
Depth: 81' - 2"
Foundation: Finished Walkout Basement

search online @ eplans.com

**Come home to true Southern glamour** in this stunning Greek Revival. Imposing columns enclose a double porch, creating a dramatic entrance. The foyer showcases a spiral staircase and opens to a formal dining room on the left and a library on the right—both warmed by fireplaces. The family will love spending quality time in the huge hearth-warmed living room, which opens to a rear triple porch. On the left of the plan, the island kitchen is expanded by a breakfast area and keeping room. Elegance abounds in the right wing, where the master suite takes center stage. The second floor is home to four spacious bedrooms—one with a fireplace—two baths, and a playroom. A balcony that opens to the second-level porch also overlooks the foyer below. The lower level of this home is its own little world, with a pub, rec room, efficiency kitchen, hobby and exercise rooms, and another full bath and bedroom.

**LOWER LEVEL**

**MAIN LEVEL**

**UPPER LEVEL**

**plan# HPK1100082**

**Style: GREEK REVIVAL**
**First Floor:** 3,902 sq. ft.
**Second Floor:** 2,159 sq. ft.
**Total:** 6,061 sq. ft.
**Bedrooms:** 5
**Bathrooms:** 3½
**Width:** 85' - 3"
**Depth:** 74' - 0"
**Foundation:** Walkout
**Basement**

**search online @ eplans.com**

**The entry to this classic home** is framed with a sweeping double staircase and four large columns topped with a pediment. The two-story foyer is flanked by spacious living and dining rooms. The two-story family room, which has a central fireplace, opens to the study and a solarium. A spacious U-shaped kitchen features a central island cooktop. An additional staircase off the breakfast room offers convenient access to the second floor. The impressive master suite features backyard access and a bath fit for royalty. Four bedrooms upstairs enjoy large proportions.

**FIRST FLOOR**

**SECOND FLOOR**

# Greek Revival Homes

## plan# HPK1100083

**Style: GREEK REVIVAL**
First Floor: 3,509 sq. ft.
Second Floor: 1,564 sq. ft.
Total: 5,073 sq. ft.
Bedrooms: 4
Bathrooms: 4½ + ½
Width: 86' - 6"
Depth: 67' - 3"
Foundation: Walkout
Basement

**search online @ eplans.com**

**Classic symmetry sets off this graceful exterior,** with two sets of double columns framed by tall windows and topped with a detailed pediment. Just off the foyer, the study and dining room present an elegant impression. The gourmet kitchen offers a food-preparation island and a lovely breakfast bay. The central gallery hall connects casual living areas with the master wing. A delightful dressing area with a split vanity and a bay window indulge the lavish master bath. The master bedroom features a bumped-out glass sitting area, a tray ceiling, and a romantic fireplace. Upstairs, three bedroom suites are pampered with private baths.

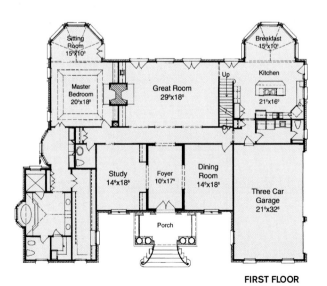

**FIRST FLOOR**

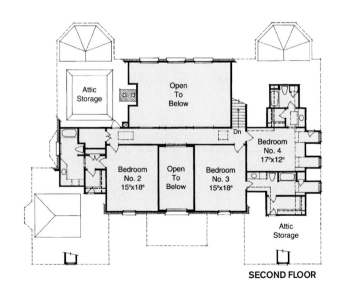

**SECOND FLOOR**

ORDER BLUEPRINTS 24 HOURS, 7 DAYS A WEEK, AT 1-800-521-6797

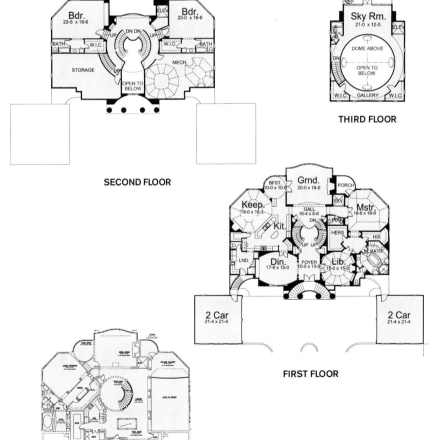

**SECOND FLOOR**

**THIRD FLOOR**

**FIRST FLOOR**

**BASEMENT**

**plan # HPK1100084**

**Style: GREEK REVIVAL**
First Floor: 3,340 sq. ft.
Second Floor: 1,540 sq. ft.
Third Floor: 850 sq. ft.
Total: 5,730 sq. ft.
Bedrooms: 3
Bathrooms: 4½
Width: 106' - 0"
Depth: 82' - 0"
Foundation: Finished Basement

**search online @ eplans.com**

**This is a grand design**—there is no denying it. Symmetrical, ornate, historical, and complex, it speaks to those with the discretion to investigate a very particular kind of estate home. Interior spaces are adorned with distinctive details. The entry and gallery focus on circular stairs with double access to the second-floor landing. Each of the living areas has a unique and decorative ceiling treatment. Even the master bath is enhanced beyond the ordinary. Aspects to appreciate: a formal library, two walk-in pantries, a master bedroom vestibule, double garages, a private master bedroom porch, an elevator, and a gigantic storage area on the second floor.

© William E. Poole Designs, Inc.

## plan# HPK1100085

**Style: GREEK REVIVAL**
First Floor: 2,473 sq. ft.
Second Floor: 1,447 sq. ft.
Total: 3,920 sq. ft.
Bonus Space: 428 sq. ft.
Bedrooms: 4
Bathrooms: 3½
Width: 68' - 8"
Depth: 80' - 0"
Foundation: Crawlspace,
Unfinished Walkout Basement
**search online @ eplans.com**

**The grand appearance** of this Greek Revival home is timeless. Inside, the family room is enhanced by a central fireplace, a built-in bookcase, and access to a rear porch. The adjacent master suite boasts His and Hers wardrobes, a whirlpool tub, a dual-sink vanity, and a private toilet and shower. The right side of the first floor features a side porch that leads to the mud room. The island kitchen will be a family favorite with wraparound counter space, a built-in desk, a walk-in pantry, and a sunporch that doubles as a breakfast area. The second floor houses a second master suite, or possible guest suite, complete with all of the amenities of the first floor master. Two additional family bedrooms share a full bath. A future rec room above the garage completes this plan.

**FIRST FLOOR**

**SECOND FLOOR**

**plan# HPK1100086**

**Southern grandeur is evident** in this wonderful two-story design with its magnificent second-floor balcony. The formal living spaces—dining room and living room—flank the impressive foyer with its stunning staircase. The family room resides in the rear, opening to the terrace. The sunny breakfast bay adjoins the island kitchen for efficient planning. The right wing holds the two-car garage, utility room, a secondary staircase, and a study that can easily be converted to a guest suite with a private bath. The master suite and Bedrooms 2 and 3 are placed on the second floor.

**Style: GREEK REVIVAL**
First Floor: 2,033 sq. ft.
Second Floor: 1,447 sq. ft.
Total: 3,480 sq. ft.
Bonus Space: 411 sq. ft.
Bedrooms: 3
Bathrooms: 3½
Width: 67' - 10"
Depth: 64' - 4"
Foundation: Crawlspace, Unfinished Basement

**search online @ eplans.com**

TERRACE AREA

2 CAR GARAGE
22'-10" X 23'-0"

STOOP

© William E. Poole Designs

BREAKFAST
9'-0" X 13'-0"

REFG. SINK D.W.

STORAGE

WASH. DRY.

SINK

FAMILY ROOM
20'-8" X 14'-8"

SINK

BAR

DESK

KITCHEN
19'-8" X 16'-2"

OVENS

STOR.

UTILITY

UP

PDR. ROOM

PANTRY

CHINA

REAR ENTRY

PORCH

LIVING ROOM
14'-0" X 15'-10"

LINE OF BALCONY

STORAGE

FOYER
14'-0" X 12'-4"

DINING ROOM
14'-0" X 14'-6"

STUDY
13'-0" X 12'-0"

BATH 2

LIN

PORCH
44'-6" X 8'-0"

**FIRST FLOOR**

ROOF AREA

WALK IN CLOSET

STORAGE

MASTER BATH

KNEE SPACE

WARDROBE

BEDROOM 2
13'-0" X 14'-8"

BATH 3

HANDRAIL

HANDRAIL

DOWN

STORAGE

FUTURE REC. ROOM
20'-10" X 15'-10"
9' CEILING BREAKLINE

MASTER BEDROOM
14'-0" X 19'-0"

OPEN TO BELOW

UP TO ATTIC

HANDRAIL

DOWN

LINE

BEDROOM 3
14'-0" X 12'-4"

UPPER FOYER

ROOF AREA

PORCH
44'-6" X 8'-0"

**SECOND FLOOR**

© William E. Poole Designs, Inc.

## plan# HPK1100087

**Style: GREEK REVIVAL**
First Floor: 2,099 sq. ft.
Second Floor: 1,260 sq. ft.
Total: 3,359 sq. ft.
Bonus Space: 494 sq. ft.
Bedrooms: 4
Bathrooms: 3½
Width: 68' - 4"
Depth: 54' - 0"
Foundation: Crawlspace

**search online @ eplans.com**

**This Colonial home gets a Victorian treatment** with an expansive covered porch complete with a gazebo-like terminus. Inside, the impressive foyer is flanked by the living room and the formal dining room. The spacious island kitchen is ideally situated between the dining room and the sunny breakfast area. Completing the living area, the family room enjoys a fireplace, built-ins, and a generous view. The lavish master suite resides on the far right with a private bath and a huge walk-in closet. A second master suite is found on the upper level, along with two additional bedrooms that share a full bath.

**FIRST FLOOR**

**SECOND FLOOR**

© William E. Poole Designs, Inc.

## plan# HPK1100088

**The grandiose entrance is reminiscent** of homes from Early America and the exquisite interior does not disappoint. Formal living areas give way to the informal openness of the family room and adjoining breakfast area and island kitchen. Access to the rear terrace from this area makes alfresco meals an option. Upstairs houses three additional family bedrooms—two share a Jack-and-Jill bath and the third boasts a private, full bath. A future rec room completes this level.

**Style: GREEK REVIVAL**
First Floor: 2,767 sq. ft.
Second Floor: 1,179 sq. ft.
Total: 3,946 sq. ft.
Bonus Space: 591 sq. ft.
Bedrooms: 4
Bathrooms: 3½ + ½
Width: 79' - 11"
Depth: 80' - 6"
Foundation: Crawlspace

**search online @ eplans.com**

**FIRST FLOOR**

**SECOND FLOOR**

# Greek Revival Homes

## plan(#) HPK1100089

Style: **GREEK REVIVAL**
First Floor: 1,282 sq. ft.
Second Floor: 956 sq. ft.
Total: 2,238 sq. ft.
Bedrooms: 2
Bathrooms: 3
Width: 30' - 2"
Depth: 74' - 2"
Foundation: Crawlspace

search online @ eplans.com

**There won't be any chilly mornings** for the homeowner within this lovely townhome. The second-floor master suite boasts a massive hearth, flanked by built-in shelves. French doors open from the bedroom to a private balcony, where gentle breezes may invigorate the senses. A gallery hall leads to a secondary bedroom, which offers its own bath and a walk-in closet. On the first floor, formal rooms share a through-fireplace and offer doors to the veranda and garden court. A secluded study easily converts to a guest suite or home office, and convenient storage space is available in the rear-loading garage.

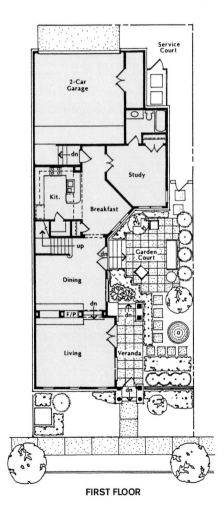

**FIRST FLOOR**

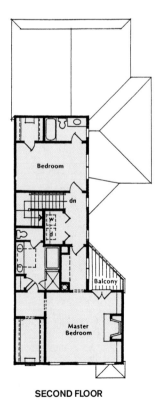

**SECOND FLOOR**

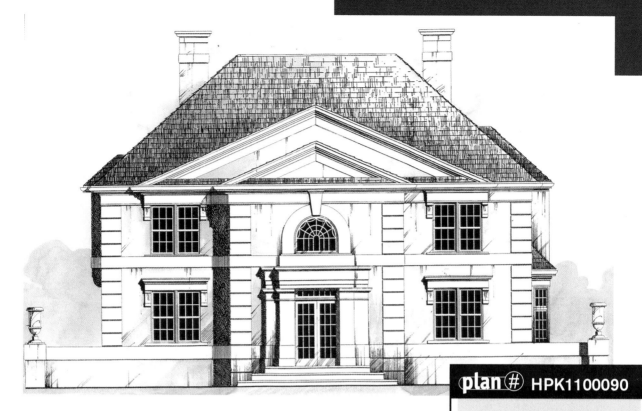

**Hints of Greek Revivalism** blend beautifully with Early American style for a handsome home with world-wide appeal. The entry is gracefully lit by a second-story arched window and leads guests into a bayed living room. The great room is ready to host any occasion, with a corner fireplace and built-in entertainment center. The kitchen has a central island and easily serves the breakfast nook and dining area. Upstairs, three bedrooms line the right side of the plan, and the master suite is on the left. Here, vaulted ceilings and walk-in closets are lovely luxuries, but the real standout is the bath, with a whirlpool tub and a see-through fireplace shared with the bedroom.

**plan# HPK1100090**

**Style: GREEK REVIVAL**
**First Floor:** 1,332 sq. ft.
**Second Floor:** 1,331 sq. ft.
**Total:** 2,663 sq. ft.
**Bedrooms:** 4
**Bathrooms:** 3½
**Width:** 48' - 0"
**Depth:** 42' - 0"
**Foundation: Unfinished Basement**

**search online @ eplans.com**

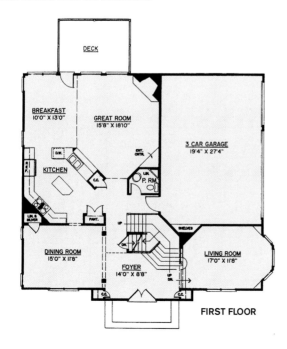

FIRST FLOOR

SECOND FLOOR

## plan # HPK1100091

**Style: GREEK REVIVAL**
First Floor: 1,807 sq. ft.
Second Floor: 1,970 sq. ft.
Total: 3,777 sq. ft.
Bedrooms: 4
Bathrooms: 3½
Width: 57' - 4"
Depth: 53' - 6"
Foundation: Unfinished
Walkout Basement

**search online @ eplans.com**

**For sheer magnificence,** this chateau-style mansion is unbeatable. Guests will be enchanted, both by the pillared entry and the inside splendor. The two-story grand room, with an extended-hearth fireplace, is well designed for unforgettable soiree's. A front dining room and living room (or make it a library) radiate a gracious welcome. The kitchen can easily serve gourmet dinners and informal family meals. It opens to an exquisite breakfast bay with five windows and to a keeping room with a fireplace. All four bedrooms are situated upstairs, and the posh master suite enjoys His and Hers walk-in closets and vanities. The laundry is conveniently located on this floor.

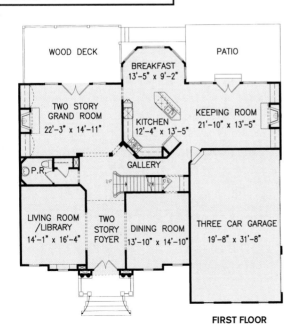

**FIRST FLOOR**

**SECOND FLOOR**

© William E. Poole Designs, Inc.

plan # HPK1100092

**Style: GREEK REVIVAL**
**First Floor:** 1,209 sq. ft.
**Second Floor:** 1,005 sq. ft.
**Total:** 2,214 sq. ft.
**Bonus Space:** 366 sq. ft.
**Bedrooms:** 3
**Bathrooms:** 2½
**Width:** 65' - 4"
**Depth:** 40' - 4"
**Foundation: Crawlspace**

search online @ eplans.com

**The rebirth of a style**—this design salutes the look of Early America. From the porch, step into the two-story foyer, and either venture to the left towards the living room and dining room, or to the right where the family room sits. A central fireplace in the family room warms the island kitchen. The open design allows unrestricted interaction. Upstairs, the master suite boasts a roomy bath with a dual-sink vanity, a whirlpool tub, a private toilet, a separate shower, and His and Hers walk-in closets. Two additional family bedrooms share a full bath. Future expansion space completes this level.

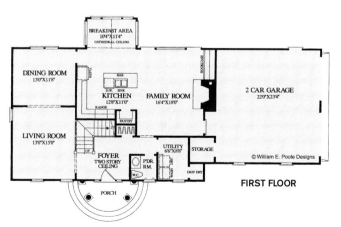

FIRST FLOOR

SECOND FLOOR

© William E. Poole Designs, Inc.

## plan# HPK1100093

**Style: GREEK REVIVAL**
First Floor: 2,320 sq. ft.
Second Floor: 1,009 sq. ft.
Total: 3,329 sq. ft.
Bonus Space: 521 sq. ft.
Bedrooms: 4
Bathrooms: 3½
Width: 80' - 4"
Depth: 58' - 0"
Foundation: Crawlspace

**search online @ eplans.com**

**Sturdy columns on a spacious,** welcoming front porch lend a Greek Revival feel to this design, and three dormer windows provide a relaxed country look. The living and dining rooms, each with a fireplace, flank the two-story foyer; the family room also includes a fireplace, as well as built-in shelves and a wall of windows. The L-shaped kitchen, conveniently near the breakfast area, features a work island and a large pantry. Two walk-in closets highlight the lavish master suite, which offers a private bath with a soothing whirlpool tub. Three family bedrooms—all with dormer alcoves and two with walk-in closets—sit upstairs, along with a future recreation room.

**FIRST FLOOR**

**SECOND FLOOR**

© William E. Poole Designs, Inc.

**plan# HPK1100094**

**This home exudes** Early American elegance. Inside, a central fireplace in the family room conveniently warms the adjacent island kitchen and cathedral-ceilinged breakfast area. A built-in entertainment center is an added bonus to this area. Upstairs, the master suite features a sitting area, a dual-sink vanity, a private toilet, whirlpool tub, separate shower, and His and Hers walk-in closets. Two additional family bedrooms share a full hall bath.

**Style: GREEK REVIVAL**
First Floor: 1,291 sq. ft.
Second Floor: 1,087 sq. ft.
Total: 2,378 sq. ft.
Bonus Space: 366 sq. ft.
Bedrooms: 3
Bathrooms: 2½
Width: 65' - 4"
Depth: 40' - 0"
Foundation: Crawlspace

search online @ eplans.com

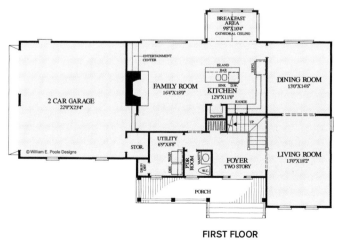

**FIRST FLOOR**

**SECOND FLOOR**

© William E. Poole Designs, Inc.

## plan # HPK1100095

**Style: GREEK REVIVAL**
First Floor: 1,688 sq. ft.
Second Floor: 630 sq. ft.
Total: 2,318 sq. ft.
Bonus Space: 506 sq. ft.
Bedrooms: 3
Bathrooms: 3½
Width: 44' - 4"
Depth: 62' - 4"
Foundation: Crawlspace,
Unfinished Walkout Basement
search online @ eplans.com

**This Southern Colonial beauty** features three porches: one welcomes visitors to the first floor, the second offers a pleasant retreat from a bedroom upstairs, and the third, a screened porch, sits at the rear of the house, accessed from the great room. A centrally located fireplace in the great room warms the entire area, including the kitchen and the breakfast room. The spacious kitchen is a family favorite with a snack bar and a scenic view of the backyard. The left side of the plan is dominated by the master suite. The master bath boasts a dual sink vanity, a whirlpool tub, a separate shower, a compartmented toilet, and His and Hers walk-in closets. Upstairs, there are two additional family bedrooms, each with a full bath. Future space on the second floor invites the possibility of a fourth bedroom and a recreation room. A two-car garage completes the plan.

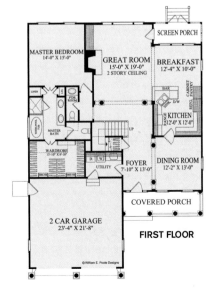

**FIRST FLOOR**

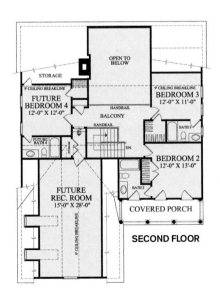

**SECOND FLOOR**

**plan# HPK1100096**

Style: **GREEK REVIVAL**
Square Footage: 2,987
Bedrooms: 3
Bathrooms: 2½
Width: 74' - 0"
Depth: 62' - 0"
Foundation: Walkout Basement

**search online @ eplans.com**

**Reaching back through the centuries** for its inspiration, this home reflects the grandeur that was ancient Rome—as it looked to newly independent Americans in the 1700s. The entry portico provides a classic twist: the balustrade that would have marched across the roofline of a typical Revival home trims to form the balcony outside the French doors of the study. Inside, the foyer opens to the study, as well as the formal dining room, then leads to a welcoming great room warmed by a fireplace. The left wing is given over to a private master suite with a bath that offers the ultimate in luxury, including a large walk-in closet. On the right side of the house, two additional bedrooms share a full bath. Separating the sleeping wings is the kitchen, with its nearby keeping/family room.

© William E. Poole Designs, Inc.

## plan # HPK1100097

**Style: GREEK REVIVAL**
Square Footage: 2,639
Bonus Space: 396 sq. ft.
Bedrooms: 3
Bathrooms: 2½
Width: 73' - 8"
Depth: 58' - 6"
Foundation: Crawlspace

search online @ eplans.com

**Colonial architecture,** like this elegant home, lends a classic air to any neighborhood. The interior offers a completely modern arrangement with the dramatic foyer opening to the spectacular living room with its window wall, cathedral ceiling, and stunning fireplace. To the left, the kitchen is central to the more intimate family/sunroom and breakfast area. The formal dining room, to the left of the foyer, completes the living area. The sleeping quarters on the right include two bedrooms and a romantic master suite with a plush private bath.

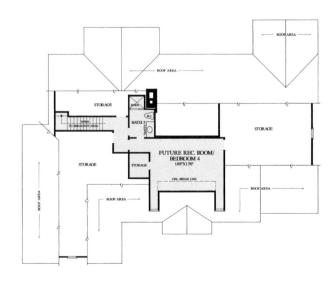

© William E. Poole Designs, Inc.

**The columned entry** of this Colonial home speaks for itself, but the inside actually seals the deal. The cooktop-island kitchen flows easily into the breakfast area and great room. The vaulted-ceiling sunroom accesses a rear covered porch perfect for outdoor entertaining. The master suite enjoys a private entrance to the rear porch, central His and Hers wardrobes, and a spacious bath. Upstairs, three family bedrooms share two full baths. Expansion space makes a future rec room an option. Extra storage space is the garage in an added convenience.

**plan# HPK1100098**

Style: **GREEK REVIVAL**
First Floor: **2,746 sq. ft.**
Second Floor: **992 sq. ft.**
Total: **3,738 sq. ft.**
Bonus Space: **453 sq. ft.**
Bedrooms: **4**
Bathrooms: **3½**
Width: **80' - 0"**
Depth: **58' - 6"**
Foundation: **Crawlspace**

search online @ eplans.com

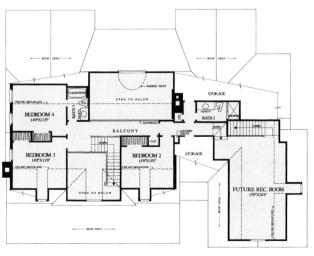

FIRST FLOOR

SECOND FLOOR

© William E. Poole Designs, Inc.

## plan# HPK1100099

**Style: GREEK REVIVAL**
First Floor: 2,449 sq. ft.
Second Floor: 1,094 sq. ft.
Total: 3,543 sq. ft.
Bonus Space: 409 sq. ft.
Bedrooms: 4
Bathrooms: 3½
Width: 89' - 0"
Depth: 53' - 10"
Foundation: Crawlspace

search online @ eplans.com

**An impressive front porch** coupled with charming twin dormers makes this home a delightful addition to any neighborhood. The sunroom doubles as a delightful area to enjoy meals, a view of the backyard, and gain access to the rear porch. The family room and living room/library each boast a private fireplace. Upstairs houses three additional bedrooms, two sharing a full bath with a dual-sink vanity and one with an attached full bath. Future expansion space and extra storage space complete the second floor.

**SECOND FLOOR**

**FIRST FLOOR**

© The Sater Design Collection, Inc.

**A careful blend of horizontal siding** and stucco accents lends a continental appeal to this voguish home. Cutting-edge style continues with an interior plan designed to accommodate traditional events as well as casual living. A grand foyer opens to two octagonal formal rooms and a gallery hall that leads to the master suite and a guest and living wing. The master suite features a dressing area with a three-way mirror, art niche, and walk-in closet designed for two. Three guest suites share two baths and a private hall with a laundry.

**plan# HPK1100100**

Style: **GREEK REVIVAL**
Square Footage: 3,215
Bedrooms: 4
Bathrooms: 3
Width: 104' - 4"
Depth: 74' - 6"
Foundation: Slab

**search online @ eplans.com**

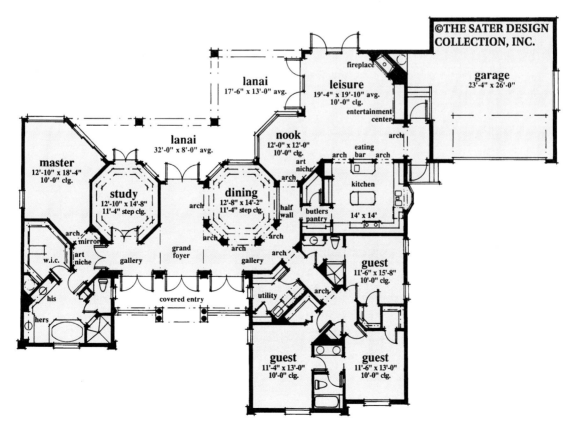

©THE SATER DESIGN COLLECTION, INC.

© William E. Poole Designs, Inc.

## plan # HPK1100101

**Style: GREEK REVIVAL**
Square Footage: 2,394
Bedrooms: 3
Bathrooms: 3
Width: 82' - 6"
Depth: 52' - 8"
Foundation: Crawlspace

**search online @ eplans.com**

**A long covered front porch** welcomes you to this attractive three-bedroom home. Inside, the foyer opens to the formal living room on the left and also leads back to the comfortable family room. Here, a fireplace, built-ins, and sliding glass doors to the rear deck make it a great place to gather. Two family bedrooms reside on the right side of the home, each with a private bath and a walk-in closet. The homeowner will surely love the master suite, which is full of amenities such as a huge walk-in closet, a whirlpool tub, and separate shower and two vanities.

© William E. Poole Designs

© William E. Poole Designs, Inc.

**With an abundance of natural light** and amenities, this home is sure to please. The sunporch doubles as a delightful area to enjoy meals with a view. A mud room off the utility room accesses a side porch and serves as a place to hang coats or shed dirty shoes before entering the kitchen or family room. The master bedroom, family room, and living room/library each boast a private fireplace. Upstairs houses three additional bedrooms, two sharing a full bath and one with an attached full bath. Future expansion space completes the second floor. Extra storage space in the garage is an added convenience.

**plan# HPK1100102**

**Style: GREEK REVIVAL**
**First Floor:** 2,337 sq. ft.
**Second Floor:** 1,016 sq. ft.
**Total:** 3,353 sq. ft.
**Bonus Space:** 394 sq. ft.
**Bedrooms:** 4
**Bathrooms:** 3½
**Width:** 66' - 2"
**Depth:** 71' - 2"
**Foundation:** Crawlspace

**search online @ eplans.com**

**FIRST FLOOR**

CARRIAGE HOUSE GARAGE
22'0"X24'0"

© William E. Poole Designs

STORAGE

UTILITY
LAUNDRY CHUTE

MUD ROOM

PORCH

W.C.

MASTER BATH

WHIRLPOOL TUB

HER WARDROBE

POWDER ROOM
W.C.

PORCH

FAMILY ROOM
19'8"X15'0"

MASTER BEDROOM
16'0"X17'0"

KITCHEN
15'0"X12'0"

PANTRY

SUNPORCH/ BREAKFAST AREA
15'0"X10'0"

DINING ROOM
15'0"X13'8"

DOWN

LIVING ROOM/ LIBRARY
16'0"X16'0"

FOYER

PORCH

**SECOND FLOOR**

FUT. REC. ROOM
16'0"X23'0"

DOWN

LAUNDRY CHUTE

ROOF AREA

ROOF AREA

BATH 4

BEDROOM 4
15'0"X12'10"

WALK IN CLOSET

BEDROOM 3
16'0"X13'0"

WALK IN CLOSET

BATH 3

ATTIC STORAGE

DOWN

OPEN TO FOYER BELOW

BEDROOM 2
16'0"X13'0"

ROOF AREA

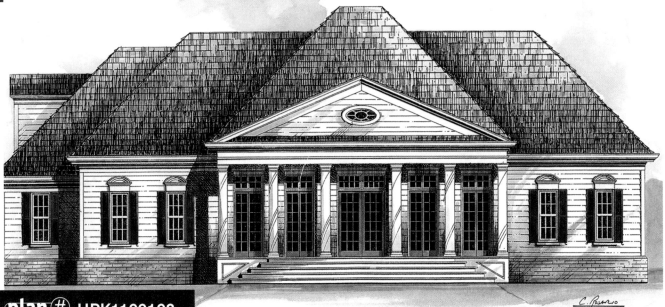

## plan# HPK1100103

**Style: GREEK REVIVAL**
First Floor: 1,684 sq. ft.
Second Floor: 776 sq. ft.
Total: 2,460 sq. ft.
Bedrooms: 4
Bathrooms: 3½
Width: 66' - 0"
Depth: 46' - 0"
Foundation: Unfinished
Basement

**search online @ eplans.com**

**The stately pillars that highlight** the facade of this Greek Revival home invite all visitors to enter into the spacious two-story foyer, beyond which lies a treasure of amenities. Both the dining room and the library, which flank the foyer, have twin sets of French doors that open onto the front porch. The huge family room with a cozy fireplace flows smoothly into the kitchen and breakfast bay. The entire right wing encompasses the master suite, truly a testimony to fine living. Upstairs, three bedrooms share two baths. Additional second-level space can be developed for expansion.

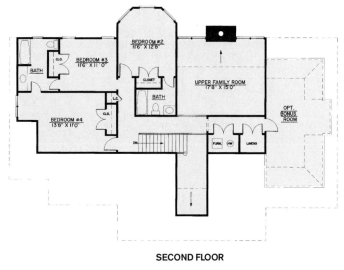

**SECOND FLOOR**

**FIRST FLOOR**

**A handsome porch dressed up** with Greek Revival details greets visitors warmly in this Early American home. The foyer opens to the airy and spacious living room and dining room with vaulted ceilings. The secluded master bedroom also sports a vaulted ceiling and is graced with a dressing area, private bath, and walk-in closet. Two decks located at the rear of the plan are accessed via the master bedroom, kitchen, and living room. A full bath serves the two family bedrooms.

plan# **HPK1100104**

Style: **GREEK REVIVAL**
Square Footage: 1,550
Bedrooms: 3
Bathrooms: 2
Width: 62' - 8"
Depth: 36' - 0"
Foundation: Unfinished Basement

search online @ eplans.com

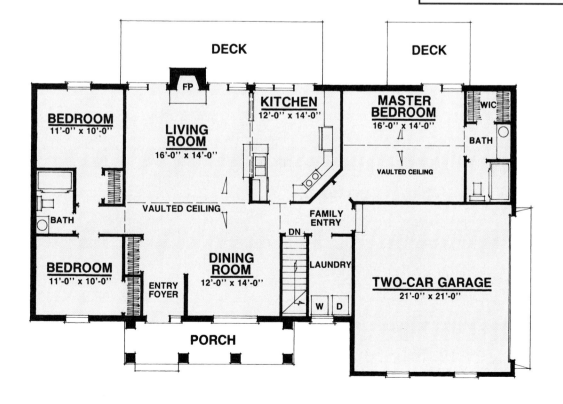

© William E. Poole Designs, Inc.

## plan# HPK1100105

**Style: GREEK REVIVAL**
**Square Footage:** 2,869
**Bedrooms:** 3
**Bathrooms:** 3½
**Width:** 68' - 6"
**Depth:** 79' - 8"
**Foundation:** Crawlspace

**search online @ eplans.com**

**Here is a beautiful example** of Classical Revival architecture complete with shuttered, jack-arch windows and a column-supported pediment over the entry. Inside, the foyer opens to the living room and leads to the family room at the rear. Here, a panoramic view is complemented by an impressive fireplace framed by built-ins. To the left, the efficient island kitchen is situated between the sunny breakfast nook and the formal dining room. The right side of the plan holds two bedrooms and the lavish master suite.

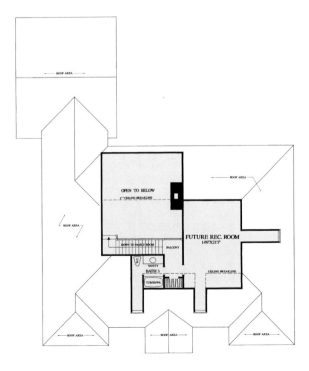

# Floridian Plans

From Native Americans to the early Spanish settlers to American Colonists, each group left its mark on Floridian home design. Today, the classic design is a combination of Mediterranean and Colonial styles that emerged in the early 1900s and incorporates the best of each influence.

Modern Floridian-style homes are usually a single story, with low roof lines and grand arches that protect the interior spaces from the semi-tropical climate. Many are quite large. Floor plans are both formal and traditionally Floridian, where outdoors and indoors are intended to operate as a generous living space.

Unique among the most common Southern-style homes, the modern Floridian is rarely symmetrical. Offset entries, sheltered from the sun, are common features, as are varied rooflines, stucco facades, and captivating colors. Enclosed courtyards are a means to create privacy and interior gardens.

With its climate, sunshine, and vast coastlines, Florida is a truly special place. The architecture it has spawned is a tribute to the whole Southern region, as appealing in Florida as it is in parts of Virginia or Maryland. ∎

**While only one story, the rooflines on this home (page 162) captivate, especially at night.**

# Grand Floridian

*Florida style is both formal and relaxed*

The Floridian-style architecture of this home is evident in its low roof lines and grand arches, and is influenced by both Mediterranean and Art Deco design. This very large home is a contemporary estate; both formal and traditionally Floridian, where outdoors and indoors are seamlessly melded together.

**A covered pool and terrace blur the distinction between interior and exterior spaces in this Floridian home, and water is the powerful visual element that connects them.**

Inviting glass-paneled doors from the porte-cochere lead to the foyer and an open interior that flows among spaces that are truly grand. Intimate spaces are defined by decorative columns, stone arches, and coffered ceilings. The large living room boasts a great fireplace, and both the formal living area and dining area have vast expanses of windows to take in the views. In addition to the public reception spaces, there is plenty of casual space for impromptu get-togethers and relaxing family gatherings. And the expansive kitchen, with its large island, is central to this informal area. ■

**Above: The living room, with its 20-foot coffered ceiling, provides stunning backyard views. Right: behind the extraordinary facade lies a wealth of fine details.**

Top: Columns make this already grand room seem even more extravagant. Above Left: Sliding walls of glass open the leisure room to the courtyard lanai. Right: Graceful curves and soaring ceilings add elegance to the master bath.

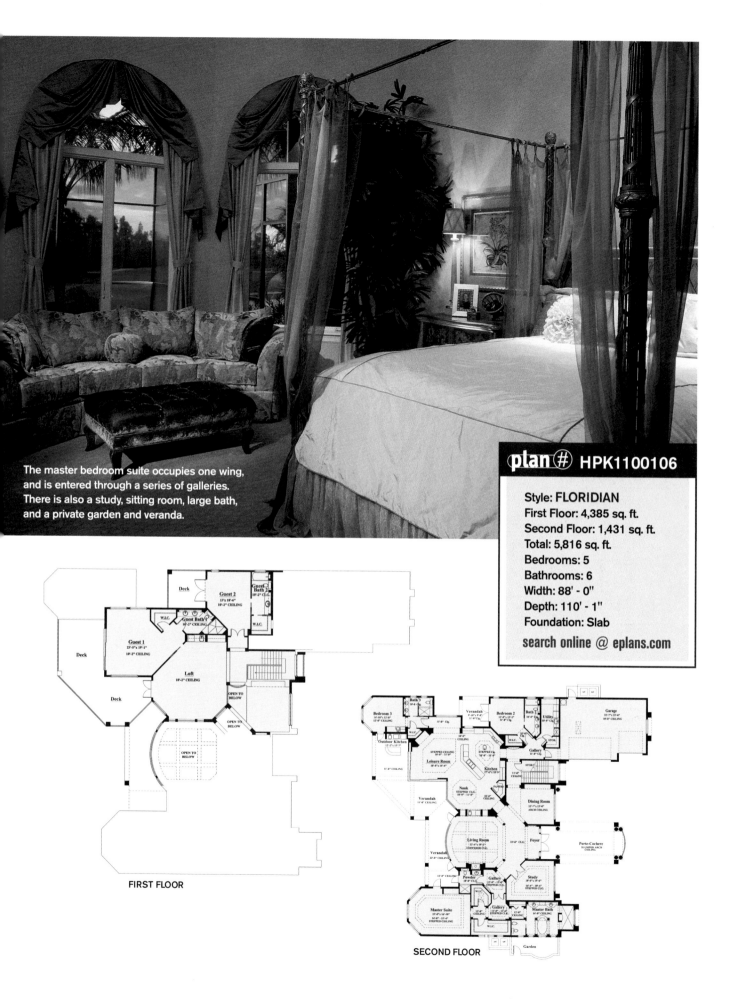

The master bedroom suite occupies one wing, and is entered through a series of galleries. There is also a study, sitting room, large bath, and a private garden and veranda.

**plan# HPK1100106**

Style: **FLORIDIAN**
First Floor: 4,385 sq. ft.
Second Floor: 1,431 sq. ft.
Total: 5,816 sq. ft.
Bedrooms: 5
Bathrooms: 6
Width: 88' - 0"
Depth: 110' - 1"
Foundation: Slab

**search online @ eplans.com**

**FIRST FLOOR**

**SECOND FLOOR**

# Floridian Plans

## plan # HPK1100107

**Style:** FLORIDIAN
**Square Footage:** 3,490
**Bedrooms:** 4
**Bathrooms:** 4
**Width:** 69' - 8"
**Depth:** 115' - 0"
**Foundation:** Slab

**search online @ eplans.com**

**This Parade of Homes award winner** has striking curb appeal with its well-balanced and detailed Mediterranean facade. The floor plan offers open, formal, and casual living areas. Plenty of natural light and views to spacious outdoor areas are provided by the use of pocketing sliding glass doors, French doors, windows, and mitered glass. This design offers four full bedrooms with four full baths. The family room features a built-in entertainment center with fireplace and is easily furnished. The functional and spacious kitchen is open to the family room and dinette.

**REAR EXTERIOR**

# Floridian Plans

**plan# HPK1100108**

**Style: FLORIDIAN**
**First Floor:** 2,853 sq. ft.
**Second Floor:** 627 sq. ft.
**Total:** 3,480 sq. ft.
**Bedrooms:** 3
**Bathrooms:** 2½
**Width:** 80' - 0"
**Depth:** 96' - 0"
**Foundation:** Slab

**search online @ eplans.com**

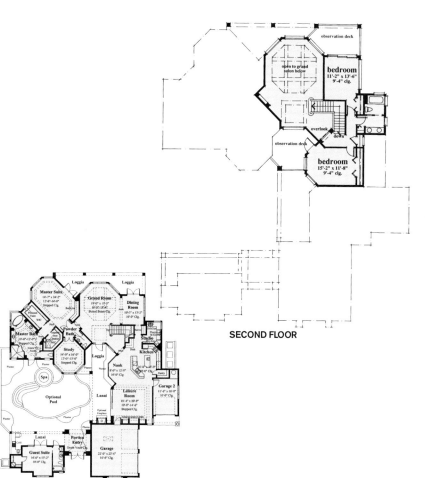

SECOND FLOOR

FIRST FLOOR

**A unique courtyard** provides a happy medium for indoor/outdoor living in this design. Inside, the foyer opens to a grand salon with a wall of glass, providing unobstructed views of the backyard. Informal areas include a leisure room with an entertainment center and glass doors that open to a covered poolside lanai. An outdoor fireplace enhances casual gatherings. The master suite is filled with amenities that include a bayed sitting area, access to the rear lanai, His and Hers closets, and a soaking tub. Upstairs, two family bedrooms—both with private decks—share a full bath. A detached guest house has a cabana bath and an outdoor grill area.

# Floridian Plans

**plan# HPK1100109**

Style: **FLORIDIAN**
Square Footage: 2,978
Bedrooms: 3
Bathrooms: 3½
Width: 84' - 0"
Depth: 90' - 0"
Foundation: Slab

search online @ eplans.com

**This home is designed to be a dream** come true. A formal living area opens from the gallery foyer through graceful arches and looks out to the veranda. The veranda hosts an outdoor grill and service counter—perfect for outdoor entertaining. The leisure room offers a private veranda, a cabana bath, and a wet bar just off the gourmet kitchen. Walls of windows and a bayed breakfast nook let in natural light and set a bright tone for this area. The master suite opens to the rear property through French doors and boasts a lavish bath with a corner whirlpool tub that overlooks a private garden. An art niche off the gallery hall, a private dressing area, and a secluded study complement the master suite. Two family bedrooms occupy the opposite wing of the plan and share a full bath and private hall.

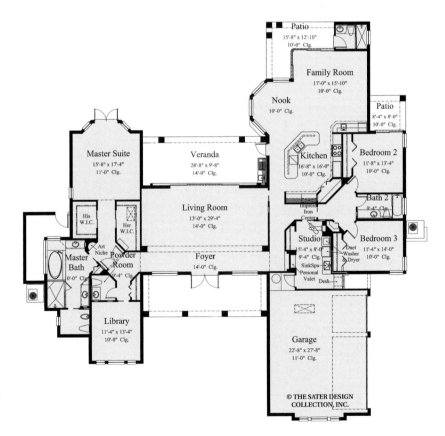

© 91 HOME DESIGN SERVICES, INC.

J.V. HANSEN

**A luxurious master suite** is just one of the highlights offered with this stunning plan—an alternate plan for this suite features a sitting room, wet bar, and fireplace. Two family bedrooms to the right share a full bath with a dual-sink vanity and a gallery hall that leads directly to the covered patio. Tile adds interest to the living area and surrounds the spacious great room, which offers a fireplace and access to the rear patio. A formal dining room and a secluded den or study flank the foyer.

**plan# HPK1100110**

Style: **FLORIDIAN**
Square Footage: 2,125
Bedrooms: 3
Bathrooms: 2
Width: 65' - 0"
Depth: 56' - 8"
Foundation: Slab

search online @ eplans.com

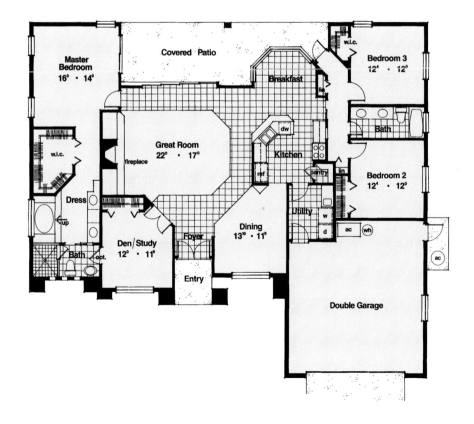

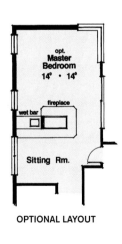

OPTIONAL LAYOUT

# Floridian Plans

**plan# HPK1100111**

Style: **FLORIDIAN**
Square Footage: 2,237
Bonus Space: 397 sq. ft.
Bedrooms: 3
Bathrooms: 2
Width: 60' - 0"
Depth: 70' - 0"
Foundation: Slab

**search online @ eplans.com**

**The elegance and grace of this split-level plan** are apparent at first sight. Impressive arches open into the foyer, with the wide-open great room beyond, opening to a covered porch through French doors. Enter both the master suite and the adjacent den/study through French doors. A private courtyard keeps the master bath shielded from the front yard. From the nook, near two good-sized bedrooms with a shared bathroom, stairs lead up to a bonus room that includes a large balcony to take advantage of your lot with a view.

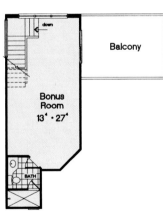

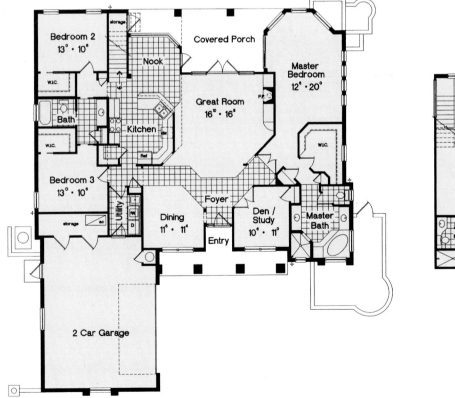

**plan# HPK1100112**

Style: **FLORIDIAN**
First Floor: 2,254 sq. ft.
Second Floor: 608 sq. ft.
Total: 2,862 sq. ft.
Bedrooms: 4
Bathrooms: 3
Width: 66' - 0"
Depth: 78' - 10"
Foundation: Slab

search online @ eplans.com

**Indoor and outdoor living** are enhanced by the beautiful courtyard that decorates the center of this home. A gallery leads to a kitchen featuring a center work island and adjacent breakfast room. To the left, the gallery leads to the formal living room and master suite. The secluded master bedroom features a tray ceiling and double doors that lead to a covered patio. The second floor contains a full bath shared by two family bedrooms and a loft that provides flexible space.

OPTIONAL LAYOUT

SECOND FLOOR

FIRST FLOOR

**plan # HPK1100113**

Style: **FLORIDIAN**
Square Footage: 1,550
Bedrooms: 3
Bathrooms: 2
Width: 43' - 0"
Depth: 59' - 0"
Foundation: Slab

**search online @ eplans.com**

**Enjoy resort-style living** in this striking Sun Country home. Guests will always feel welcome when entertained in the formal living and dining areas, but the eat-in country kitchen overlooking the family room will be the center of attention. Enjoy casual living in the large family room and out on the patio with the help of an optional summer kitchen and a view of the fairway. Built-in shelves and an optional media center provide decorating options. The master suite features a volume ceiling and a spacious master bath.

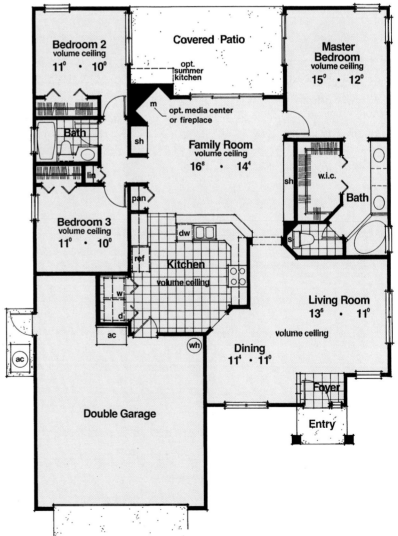

Bedroom 2
volume ceiling
11⁰ · 10⁰

Covered Patio

opt. summer kitchen

Master Bedroom
volume ceiling
15⁰ · 12⁰

Bath

m — opt. media center or fireplace

sh

lin

Family Room
volume ceiling
16⁸ · 14⁴

sh

w.i.c.

Bath

pan

Bedroom 3
volume ceiling
11⁰ · 10⁰

ref

dw

Kitchen
volume ceiling

s

w

d

ac

wh

Living Room
13⁶ · 11⁰
volume ceiling

Dining
11⁴ · 11⁰

ac

Double Garage

Foyer

Entry

**A different and exciting floor plan** defines this three-bedroom home. Clear and simple rooflines and a large welcoming entryway make it unique. A large archway frames the dining-room entry to the gallery hall. The hall leads past the kitchen toward the informal leisure and nook areas. High glass above the built-in fireplace allows for natural light and rear views. Greenhouse-style garden windows light the nook. The large master suite contains a morning kitchen and a sitting area. The bath features a make-up space, walk-in shower, and private garden tub. The two-car garage enters the home through a vast utility room that provides a large folding table.

**plan# HPK1100114**

Style: FLORIDIAN
Square Footage: 2,762
Bedrooms: 3
Bathrooms: 2½
Width: 74' - 0"
Depth: 77' - 0"
Foundation: Slab

**search online @ eplans.com**

# Floridian Plans

HOLZHAUER INC.

## plan# HPK1100115

Style: **FLORIDIAN**
Square Footage: **2,977**
Bedrooms: **3**
Bathrooms: **3**
Width: **75' - 6"**
Depth: **86' - 6"**
Foundation: **Slab**

**search online @ eplans.com**

**Behold the intricate design** of this one-story masterpiece. Amenities abound in this luxurious layout—with lavish ceiling treatments throughout and built-ins galore—this home is replete with fine details. The openness and extensive outdoor living space make entertaining an option. With space for an optional pool and pool deck, relaxation is only steps away. Ideal for the empty-nester, two guest bedrooms welcome visiting children or friends.

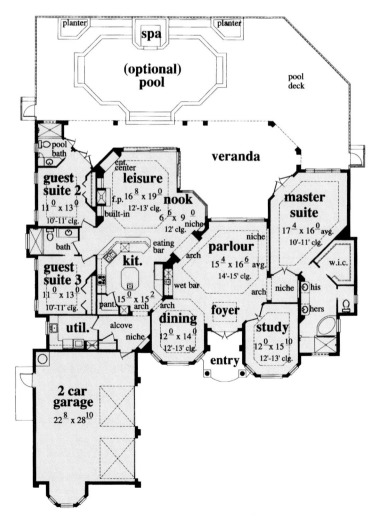

# Floridian Plans

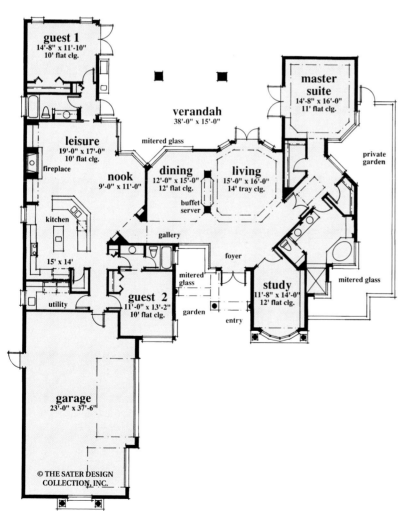

**plan# HPK1100116**

**Style: FLORIDIAN** L
**Square Footage: 2,794**
**Bedrooms: 3**
**Bathrooms: 3**
**Width: 70' - 0"**
**Depth: 98' - 0"**
**Foundation: Slab**

**search online @ eplans.com**

**Classic columns, circle-head windows,** and a bay-windowed study give this stucco home a wonderful street presence. The foyer leads to the formal living and dining areas. An arched buffet server separates these rooms and contributes an open feeling. The kitchen, nook, and leisure room are grouped for informal living. A desk/message center in the island kitchen, art niches in the nook, and a fireplace with an entertainment center and shelves add custom touches. Two secondary suites have guest baths and offer full privacy from the master wing. The master suite hosts a private garden area; the bath features a walk-in shower that overlooks the garden and a water closet room with space for books or a television. Large His and Hers walk-in closets complete these private quarters.

# Floridian Plans

## plan# HPK1100117

**Style: FLORIDIAN**
First Floor: 3,734 sq. ft.
Second Floor: 418 sq. ft.
Total: 4,152 sq. ft.
Bedrooms: 3
Bathrooms: 4½
Width: 82' - 0"
Depth: 107' - 0"
Foundation: Slab

**search online @ eplans.com**

Softly angled turrets add sweet drama to this dreamy Mediterranean manor, as a rambling interior plays function to everyday life. Beautiful interior columns in the foyer offer a fine introduction to open, spacious rooms. A secluded master suite features a beautiful bay window, a coffered ceiling, and French doors to the lanai. Across the master foyer, the private bath satisfies the homeowners' needs by offering a whirlpool tub, separate shower, private vanities, and two walk-in closets. Bedroom 2 includes a sitting bay, a walk-in closet, and a private bath. Upstairs, a spacious loft offers room for computers and books. A wet bar, walk-in closet, and full bath with a shower provide the possibility of converting this area to a bedroom suite.

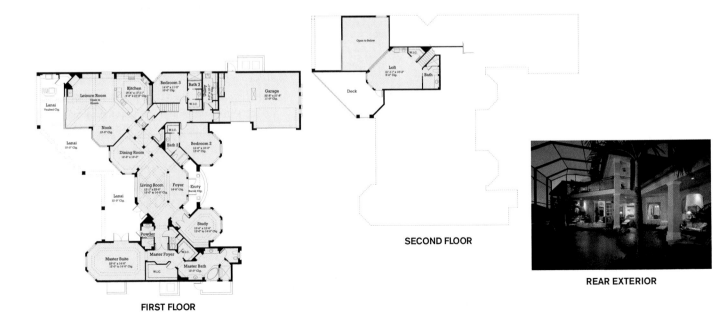

**FIRST FLOOR**

**SECOND FLOOR**

**REAR EXTERIOR**

ORDER BLUEPRINTS 24 HOURS, 7 DAYS A WEEK, AT 1-800-521-6797

© The Sater Design Collection, Inc.

## plan ⊕ HPK1100118

**Style: FLORIDIAN**
**Square Footage: 3,265**
**Bedrooms: 4**
**Bathrooms: 3½**
**Width: 80' - 0"**
**Depth: 103' - 8"**
**Foundation: Slab**

**search online @ eplans.com**

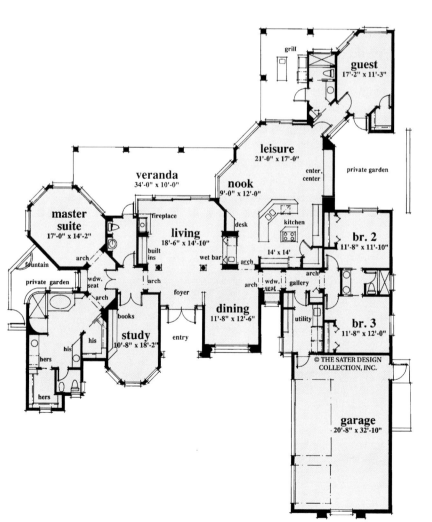

**A turret study and a raised entry** add elegance to this marvelous stucco home. The master suite has its own foyer with a window seat overlooking a private garden and fountain area; the private master bath holds dual closets, a garden tub, and a curved-glass shower. Diverse living space is the key to this plan's appeal: entertain in the living and dining rooms, enjoy family time in the leisure room, and get some privacy in the study. A guest suite includes a full bath, porch access, and a private garden entry, making it perfect for use as an in-law suite. Secondary bedrooms share a full bath.

# Floridian Plans

## plan# HPK1100119

**Style: FLORIDIAN**
Square Footage: 2,293
Bonus Space: 509 sq. ft.
Bedrooms: 3
Bathrooms: 2
Width: 51' - 0"
Depth: 79' - 4"
Foundation: Slab

**search online @ eplans.com**

**Multiple rooflines, shutters, and a charming** vaulted entry lend interest and depth to the exterior of this well-designed three-bedroom home. Inside, double doors to the left open to a cozy den. The dining room, open to the family room and foyer, features a stunning ceiling design. A fireplace and patio access and view adorn the family room. Two family bedrooms share a double-sink bathroom to the right, and the master bedroom resides to the left. Note the private patio access, two walk-in closets, and luxurious bath that ensure a restful retreat for the homeowner.

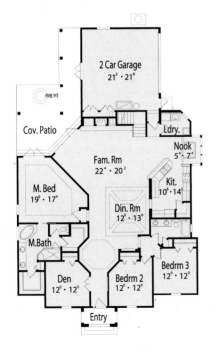

**REAR EXTERIOR**

ORDER BLUEPRINTS 24 HOURS, 7 DAYS A WEEK, AT 1-800-521-6797

**Essentially a one-story home,** the bulk of the amenities can be found on the first floor. The kitchen and breakfast area adjoin the family room, which leads to two of the four bedrooms. On the opposite side of the plan, the roomy master suite offers two walk-in closets, a garden tub, a separate shower, dual vanities, and access to the covered patio. The second story houses the fourth family bedroom complete with a full bath and a walk-in closet. A side-loading three-car garage adds appeal.

**plan # HPK1100120**

**Style: FLORIDIAN**
First Floor: 2,898 sq. ft.
Second Floor: 441 sq. ft.
Total: 3,339 sq. ft.
Bedrooms: 4
Bathrooms: 4
Width: 80' - 0"
Depth: 67' - 0"
Foundation: Slab

**search online @ eplans.com**

**FIRST FLOOR**

**SECOND FLOOR**

# Floridian Plans

## plan # HPK1100121

**Style: FLORIDIAN**
**First Floor:** 2,212 sq. ft.
**Second Floor:** 675 sq. ft.
**Total:** 2,887 sq. ft.
**Bedrooms:** 3
**Bathrooms:** 3
**Width:** 70' - 8"
**Depth:** 74' - 10"
**Foundation:** Slab

**search online @ eplans.com**

**As you drive up to the porte-cochere** entry of this home, the visual movement of the elevation is breathtaking. The multiroofed spaces bring excitement the moment you walk through the double-doored entry. The foyer leads into the wide, glass-walled living room. To the right, the formal dining room features a tiered pedestal ceiling. To the left is the guest and master suite wing of the home. The master suite, with its sweeping, curved glass wall, has access to the patio area and overlooks the pool. The master bath, with its huge walk-in closet, comes complete with a columned vanity area, a soaking tub, and a shower for two.

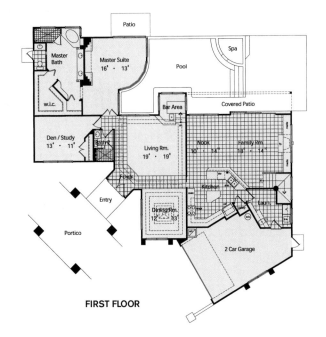

**FIRST FLOOR**

**SECOND FLOOR**

**REAR EXTERIOR**

ORDER BLUEPRINTS 24 HOURS, 7 DAYS A WEEK, AT 1-800-521-6797

# Floridian Plans

## plan # HPK1100122

**Style:** Floridian
**Square Footage:** 3,370
**Bonus Space:** 630 sq. ft.
**Bedrooms:** 3
**Bathrooms:** 4
**Width:** 74' - 6"
**Depth:** 109' - 6"
**Foundation:** Slab

search online @ eplans.com

**This stunning home won** the Parade of Homes award for Best Architectural Design. It features a unique balance of coziness and elegance. The floor plan flows flawlessly without compromising privacy or style. Natural views and outdoor living spaces enhance the open, spacious feeling inside this home. The overall layout and flow of the house and coffered ceilings maximize daylight while reflecting grandeur and richness. A pass-through wet bar may also be used as a butler's pantry. The loft above the garage is a fun and logical use of space for a second-floor game room or media room. The gourmet kitchen is superior in design and convenience. The dropped coffered ceiling in the kitchen provides intimate recessed lighting and a wonderful place to display art and kitchen decor.

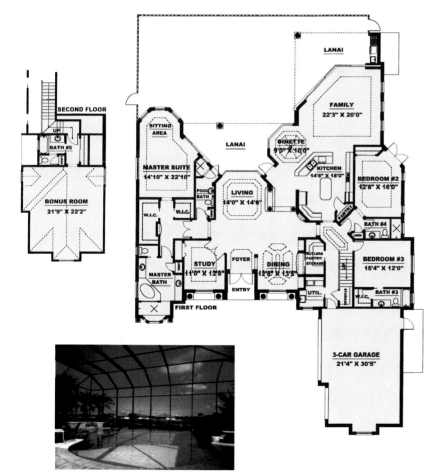

**REAR EXTERIOR**

© The Sater Design Collection, Inc.

## plan# HPK1100123

Style: **FLORIDIAN**
Square Footage: 2,385
Bonus Space: 1,271 sq. ft.
Bedrooms: 3
Bathrooms: 2½
Width: 60' - 4"
Depth: 59' - 4"
Foundation: Slab

search online @ eplans.com

**A classic pediment and low-pitched roof** are topped by a cupola on this gorgeous coastal design, influenced by 19th-Century Caribbean plantation houses. Savory style blended with a contemporary seaside spirit invites entertaining as well as year-round living—plus room to grow. The beauty and warmth of natural light splash the spacious living area with a sense of the outdoors and a touch of joie de vivre. The great room features a wall of built-ins designed for even the most technology-savvy entertainment buff. Dazzling views through walls of glass are enlivened by the presence of a breezy porch. The master suite features a luxurious bath, a dressing area, and two walk-in closets. Glass doors open to the porch and provide generous views of the seascape; a nearby study offers an indoor retreat.

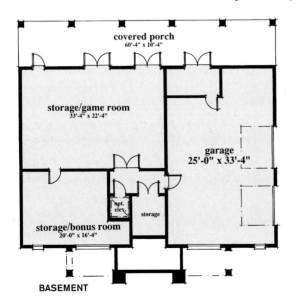

**BASEMENT**

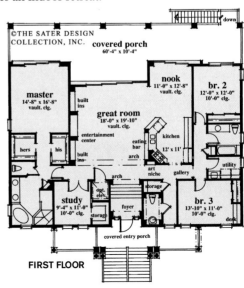

**FIRST FLOOR**

**If entertaining is your passion,** then this is the design for you. With a large, open floor plan and an array of amenities, every gathering will be a success. The foyer embraces living areas accented by a glass fireplace and a wet bar. The grand room and dining room each access a screened veranda for outside enjoyments. The gourmet kitchen delights with its openness to the rest of the house. A morning nook here also adds a nice touch. Two bedrooms and a study radiate from the first-floor living areas. Upstairs is a masterful master suite. It contains a huge walk-in closet, a whirlpool tub, and a private sundeck with a spa.

**plan# HPK1100124**

Style: **FLORIDIAN**
First Floor: 2,066 sq. ft.
Second Floor: 809 sq. ft.
Total: 2,875 sq. ft.
Bonus Space: 1,260 sq. ft.
Bedrooms: 3
Bathrooms: 3½
Width: 64' - 0"
Depth: 45' - 0"
Foundation: Pier
(same as Piling)

**search online @ eplans.com**

**REAR EXTERIOR**

**BASEMENT**

**FIRST FLOOR**

**SECOND FLOOR**

# Floridian Plans

## plan# HPK1100125

**Style: FLORIDIAN**
First Floor: 4,351 sq. ft.
Second Floor: 1,200 sq. ft.
Total: 5,551 sq. ft.
Bedrooms: 4
Bathrooms: 5½
Width: 90' - 1"
Depth: 114' - 3"
Foundation: Slab

**search online @ eplans.com**

**Graceful rooflines and a unique porte cochere** complement a vaulted entry that suggests the grand, luxurious feel that fills this spectacular 21st-Century design. Inside, the ease and comfort of a modern home project a uniquely chic attitude. Casual and formal rooms use the outdoor areas to extend the home's living space and take advantage of views through walls of glass. A first-floor guest suite has a private porch and a bath that serves as a pool cabana. The master suite features a built-in niche, glass doors to the veranda, and a stunning sitting retreat that's brightened by a bay window. A stairway and an adjacent elevator both lead upstairs to the secondary sleeping quarters. Above the garage, a bonus room with two dormer windows, a corner walk-in closet, built-ins, and a full bath offer the possibility of a fourth bedroom, home office, mother-in-law suite, or recreation space.

**REAR EXTERIOR**

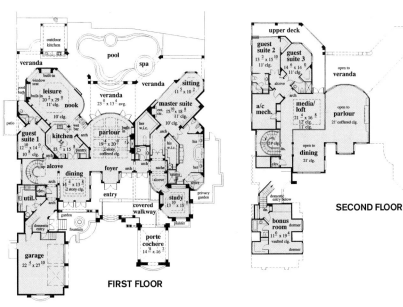

**FIRST FLOOR**

**SECOND FLOOR**

**plan# HPK1100126**

Style: **FLORIDIAN**
First Floor: 3,148 sq. ft.
Second Floor: 2,055 sq. ft.
Total: 5,203 sq. ft.
Bedrooms: 4
Bathrooms: 4½
Width: 75' - 4"
Depth: 73' - 9"

**search online @ eplans.com**

**Sun-washed Mediterranean style** offers up a luxurious and intriguing interior and exterior details. An entry porch opens to a long arcade that borders a private courtyard. The spacious gallery greets visitors with a high-style circular staircase and unobstructed views of the formal dining room and attractive study. To the right, relax in solitude and grandeur as the master suite pampers you with ornate ceilings, a sitting bay, His and Hers dressing areas, separate shower and tub, and a room-sized walk-in closet. Splendid open spaces enhance interaction between the family room and large kitchen, which feature an adjoining eating area and planning center. A convenient wine room is a gourmet delight. Generous secondary bedrooms each feature a large walk-in closet, private bath, and access to a flexible game room and tower.

FIRST FLOOR

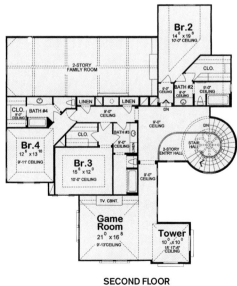

SECOND FLOOR

# Floridian Plans

© The Sater Design Collection, Inc.

## plan # HPK1100127

**Style: FLORIDIAN**
First Floor: 2,725 sq. ft.
Second Floor: 1,418 sq. ft.
Total: 4,143 sq. ft.
Bedrooms: 4
Bathrooms: 5½
Width: 61' - 4"
Depth: 62' - 0"
Foundation: Island Basement

**search online @ eplans.com**

**Florida living takes off** in this inventive design. A grand room gains attention as a superb entertaining area. A see-through fireplace here connects this room to the dining room. In the study, quiet time is assured—or slip out the doors and onto the veranda for a breather. A full bath connects the study and Bedroom 2. Bedroom 3 sits on the opposite side of the house and enjoys its own bath. The kitchen features a large work island and a connecting breakfast nook. Upstairs, the master bedroom suite contains His and Hers baths, a see-through fireplace, and access to an upper deck. A guest bedroom suite is located on the other side of the upper floor.

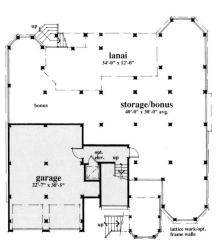

BASEMENT

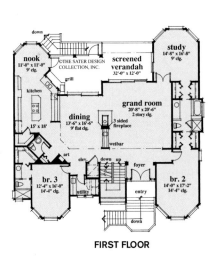

FIRST FLOOR

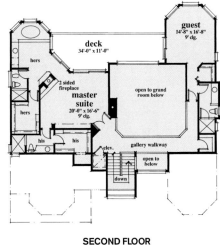

SECOND FLOOR

# Floridian Plans

**plan# HPK1100128**

**Style:** FLORIDIAN
**Square Footage:** 3,477
**Bedrooms:** 3
**Bathrooms:** 3½
**Width:** 95' - 0"
**Depth:** 88' - 8"
**Foundation:** Slab

**search online @ eplans.com**

**Make dreams come true** with this fine sunny design. An octagonal study provides a nice focal point both inside and out. The living areas remain open to each other and access outdoor areas. A wet bar makes entertaining a breeze, especially with a window pass-through to a grill area on the lanai. The kitchen enjoys shared space with a lovely breakfast nook and a bright leisure room. Two bedrooms are located near the family living center. In the master bedroom suite, luxury abounds with a two-way fireplace, a morning kitchen, two walk-in closets, and a compartmented bath. Another full bath accommodates a pool area.

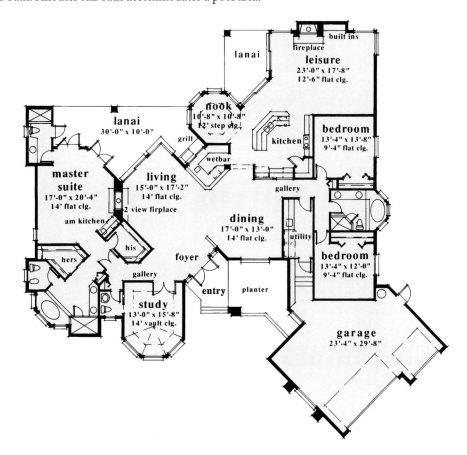

# Floridian Plans

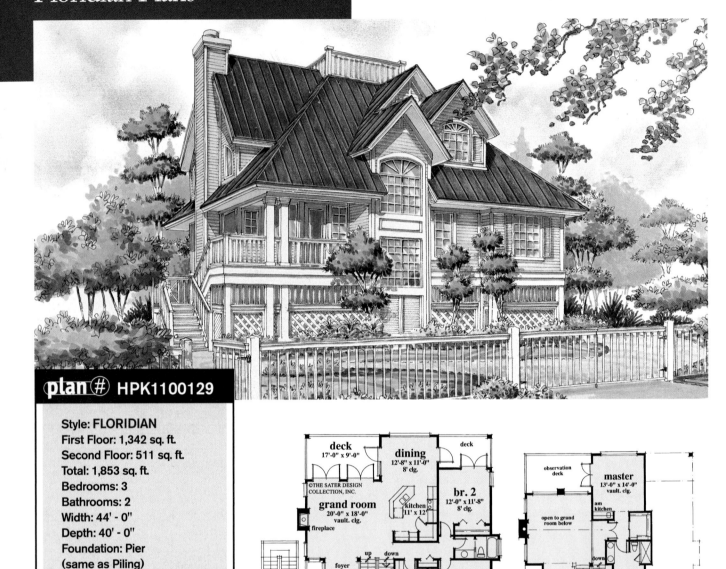

## plan # HPK1100129

Style: **FLORIDIAN**
First Floor: 1,342 sq. ft.
Second Floor: 511 sq. ft.
Total: 1,853 sq. ft.
Bedrooms: 3
Bathrooms: 2
Width: 44' - 0"
Depth: 40' - 0"
Foundation: Pier
(same as Piling)

search online @ eplans.com

**deck**
17'-0" x 9'-0"

deck

**dining**
12'-8" x 11'-0"
8' clg.

©THE SATER DESIGN COLLECTION, INC.

**grand room**
20'-0" x 18'-0"
vault. clg.

fireplace

**kitchen**
11' x 12'

**br. 2**
12'-0" x 11'-8"
8' clg.

foyer

up   down

**br. 3**
12'-0" x 10'-0"
8' clg.

down

entry porch

**FIRST FLOOR**

observation deck

**master**
13'-0" x 14'-0"
vault. clg.

am kitchen

open to grand room below

down

**SECOND FLOOR**

**Amenities abound** in this delightful two-story home. The foyer opens directly into the fantastic grand room, which offers a warming fireplace and two sets of double doors to the rear deck. The dining room also accesses this deck and a second deck shared with Bedroom 2. A convenient kitchen and another bedroom also reside on this level. Upstairs, the master bedroom reigns supreme. Entered through double doors, it pampers with a luxurious bath, walk-in closet, morning kitchen, and private observation deck.

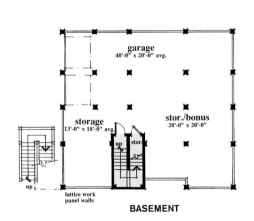

**garage**
40'-0" x 20'-0" avg.

**storage**
13'-0" x 18'-0" avg.

**stor./bonus**
20'-0" x 20'-0"

up   stor.

up

lattice work
panel walls

**BASEMENT**

search online @ eplans.com

**plan# HPK1100130**

Style: **FLORIDIAN**
First Floor: 1,235 sq. ft.
Second Floor: 1,111 sq. ft.
Total: 2,346 sq. ft.
Bedrooms: 4
Bathrooms: 3
Width: 47' - 0"
Depth: 50' - 0"
Foundation: Crawlspace,
Unfinished Basement

**A portico entrance opens to** a dramatic two-story foyer. The landing of the angled staircase is the perfect vantage point to view the vaulted living and dining rooms. Angles continue to add interest from the kitchen and breakfast bay through to the family room. The master suite includes a sunlit sitting bay, a deep closet ensuite with a raised whirlpool tub, and separate toilet and shower room.

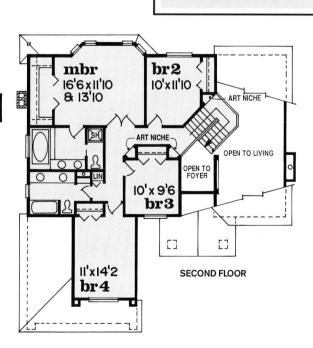

FIRST FLOOR

WALL OVER

brk
9' x 9'

VAULTED **din**
12' x 11'

k
11'10 x 12'6

14' x 14'6
**fam**

ART NICHE

**ldr**

LINE OF
2ND FLOOR
FOYER

ARCH

10' x 9'6
**den**

12' x 16'
**liv** VAULTED

19' x 20'
**two-car
garage**

SECOND FLOOR

**mbr**
16'6 x 11'10
& 13'10

**br2**
10' x 11'10

ART NICHE

ART NICHE

OPEN TO LIVING

OPEN TO
FOYER

10' x 9'6
**br3**

11' x 14'2
**br4**

# Floridian Plans

## plan # HPK1100131

**Style: FLORIDIAN**
First Floor: 2,591 sq. ft.
Second Floor: 1,399 sq. ft.
Total: 3,990 sq. ft.
Bedrooms: 4
Bathrooms: 3½
Width: 61' - 4"
Depth: 75' - 0"
Foundation: Slab

**search online @ eplans.com**

**A dramatic front stairway announces visitors** and welcomes all onto a cozy covered porch. The foyer introduces the living room on the right and the dining area on the left. Straight ahead, the family room boasts a fireplace. The kitchen is set between the breakfast room and a petite outdoor porch—perfect for grilling. Secluded on the first floor for privacy, the master suite includes two luxuriously-sized walk-in closets, private access to the rear deck, and a master bath with access to another porch out front. Upstairs, dormers enhance sunlight in two family bedrooms that share a full bath between them. A third bedroom uses the hall bath.

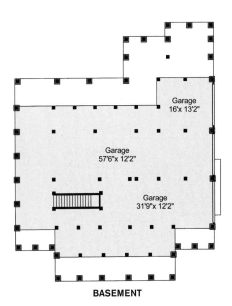

**BASEMENT**

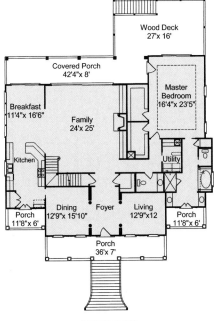

**FIRST FLOOR**

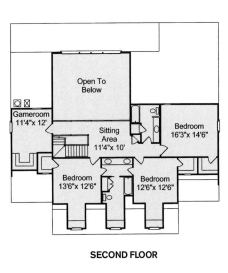

**SECOND FLOOR**

# Floridian Plans

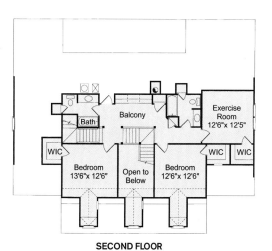

**A raised porch welcomes guests** and homeowners to relax in this four-bedroom design. French doors let in fresh breezes and allow entry to the dining room and guest bedroom on the first floor. The master bedroom sits to the right of the plan and enjoys deck and rear-porch access as well as a private front porch. The kitchen also features a private porch and adjoins a sunlit breakfast nook. A fireplace with built-ins adorns the living room. Two family bedrooms, two baths, and an exercise room fill the second floor.

**plan # HPK1100132**

Style: Floridian
First Floor: 2,213 sq. ft.
Second Floor: 1,010 sq. ft.
Total: 3,223 sq. ft.
Bedrooms: 4
Bathrooms: 4
Width: 61' - 4"
Depth: 67' - 0"
Foundation: Pier
(same as Piling)

search online @ eplans.com

**FIRST FLOOR**

Deck 27'x 12'
Porch 30'x 8'
Breakfast 11'3"x 16'6"
Master Bedroom 16'4"x 16'6"
Living Room 24'x 17'4"
Util.
WIC
WIC
Kitchen 11'3"x 19'
Bath
Ma. Bath
Porch 11'8"x 6'
Dining Room 13'3"x 13'10"
Guest Bedroom 12'6"x 12'
Porch 11'8"x 6'
Porch 26'x 7'

**SECOND FLOOR**

Bath
Balcony
Exercise Room 12'6"x 12'5"
WIC
WIC
WIC
Bedroom 13'6"x 12'6"
Open to Below
Bedroom 12'6"x 12'6"

**plan# HPK1100133**

Style: **FLORIDIAN**
Main Level: 1,677 sq. ft.
Lower Level Entry: 40 sq. ft.
Total: 1,717 sq. ft.
Bedrooms: 3
Bathrooms: 2
Width: 50' - 0"
Depth: 39' - 4"
Foundation: Unfinished
Walkout Basement

search online @ eplans.com

**This elegant home makes the most of the hillside lot** by using the lower level for a two-car garage and expandable basement space. A striking stair leads to the entry where another half-flight continues up inside. The vaulted dining room has an open rail that overlooks the entry. A vaulted ceiling in the great room accents the fireplace. A modified galley kitchen provides a snack bar and a breakfast nook. The master suite features a sitting room, compartmented bath, and walk-in closet. Two family bedrooms share a full hall bath.

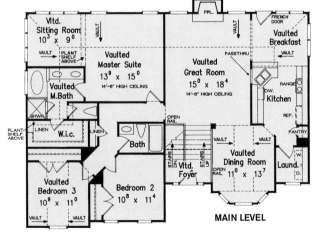

MAIN LEVEL

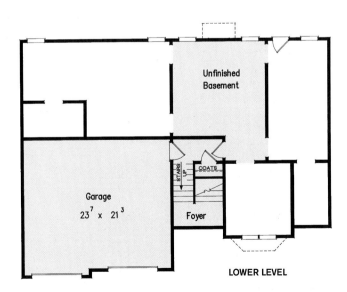

LOWER LEVEL

**plan# HPK1100134**

Style: **FLORIDIAN**
First Floor: 2,044 sq. ft.
Second Floor: 896 sq. ft.
Total: 2,940 sq. ft.
Bonus Space: 197 sq. ft.
Bedrooms: 4
Bathrooms: 3½
Width: 63' - 0"
Depth: 54' - 0"
Foundation: Unfinished
Walkout Basement, Slab,
Crawlspace

**search online @ eplans.com**

**A gracious front porch** off the formal dining room and a two-story entry set the tone for this elegant home. The living room is set to the front of the plan, thoughtfully separated from casual family areas that radiate from the kitchen. The two-story family room is framed by a balcony hall and accented with a fireplace and serving bar. The first-floor master suite features a sitting area, lush bath, and walk-in closet. Upstairs, two family bedrooms share a full bath; a third enjoys a private bath.

**FIRST FLOOR**

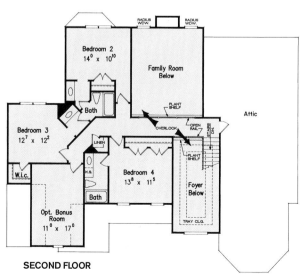

**SECOND FLOOR**

# Floridian Plans

## plan# HPK1100135

**Style: FLORIDIAN**
**Square Footage: 1,715**
**Bedrooms: 3**
**Bathrooms: 2**
**Width: 55' - 0"**
**Depth: 49' - 0"**
**Foundation: Unfinished Walkout Basement, Slab, Crawlspace**

**search online @ eplans.com**

**A grand double bank of windows** looking in on the formal dining room mirrors the lofty elegance of the extra-tall vaulted ceiling inside. From the foyer, an arched entrance to the great room visually frames the fireplace on the back wall. The wraparound kitchen has plenty of counter and cabinet space, along with a handy serving bar. The luxurious master suite features a front sitting room for quiet times and a large spa-style bath. Two family bedrooms share a hall bath.

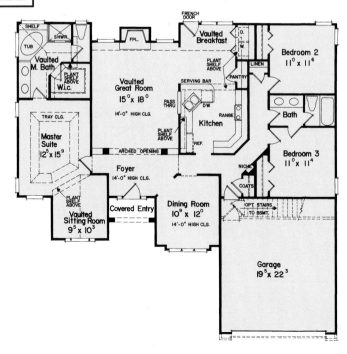

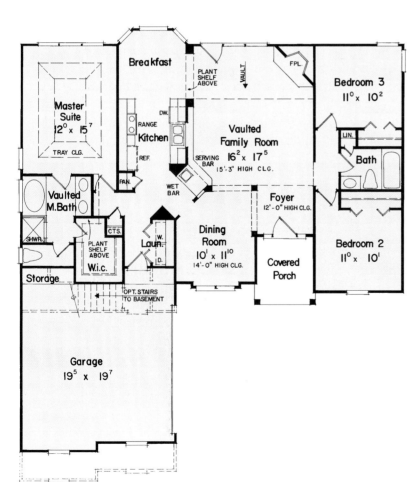

**plan # HPK1100136**

**Style: FLORIDIAN**
**Square Footage: 1,429**
**Bedrooms: 3**
**Bathrooms: 2**
**Width: 49' - 0"**
**Depth: 53' - 0"**
**Foundation: Slab, Unfinished**
**Walkout Basement,**
**Crawlspace**

**search online @ eplans.com**

**This home's gracious exterior** is indicative of the elegant yet extremely livable floor plan inside. Volume ceilings that crown the family living areas combine with an open floor plan to give the modest square footage a more spacious feel. The formal dining room is set off from the foyer and vaulted family room with stately columns. The spacious family room has a corner fireplace, rear-yard door, and serving bar from the open galley kitchen. A bay-windowed breakfast nook flanks the kitchen on one end, and a laundry center and wet bar/serving pantry leads to the dining room on the other. The split-bedroom plan allows the amenity-rich master suite maximum privacy. A pocket door off the family room leads to the hall housing the two family bedrooms and a full bath.

# Floridian Plans

## plan# HPK1100137

**Style: FLORIDIAN**
**Square Footage:** 1,670
**Bedrooms:** 3
**Bathrooms:** 2
**Width:** 54' - 0"
**Depth:** 52' - 0"
**Foundation:** Crawlspace,
**Unfinished Walkout**
**Basement, Slab**

**search online @ eplans.com**

**A grand front window display illuminates** the formal dining room and the great room of this French Country charmer. Open planning allows for easy access between the formal dining room, great room, vaulted breakfast nook, and kitchen. Extra amenities include a decorative column, fireplace, and an optional bay window in the breakfast nook. The elegant master suite is fashioned with a tray ceiling in the bedroom, a vaulted bath, and a walk-in closet. Two family bedrooms are designated by a pocket-door hall and share a large hall bath.

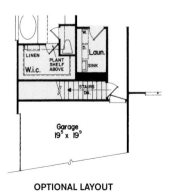

**OPTIONAL LAYOUT**

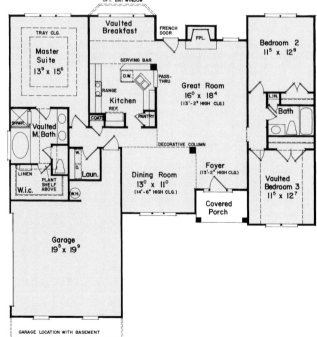

The use of stone and stucco has created a very pleasant exterior that would fit in well with a traditional environment. The double-door entry, which leads to the foyer, welcomes guests to a formal living and dining room area. Upon entering the master suite through double doors, the master bed wall becomes the focal point. A stepped ceiling treatment adds excitement, with floor-length windows framing the bed. The sitting area created by the bayed door wall further enhances the opulence of the suite. The master bath comes complete with His and Hers walk-in closets, dual vanities with a makeup area, and a soaking tub balanced by the large shower and private toilet chamber.

plan# HPK1100138

Style: **FLORIDIAN**
Square Footage: 2,755
Bonus Space: 440 sq. ft.
Bedrooms: 4
Bathrooms: 3
Width: 73' - 0"
Depth: 82' - 8"
Foundation: Slab
**search online @ eplans.com**

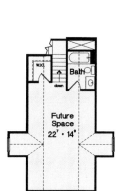

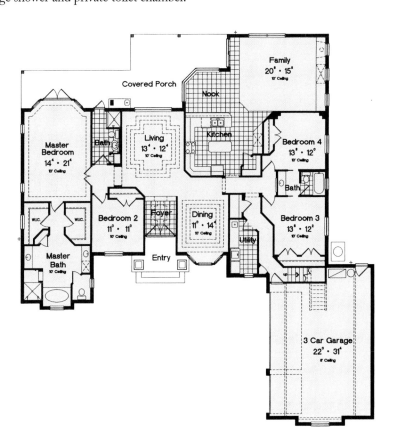

# Floridian Plans

## plan# HPK1100139

Style: Floridian
Square Footage: 3,725
Bonus Space: 595 sq. ft.
Bedrooms: 3
Bathrooms: 3½
Width: 84' - 3"
Depth: 115' - 2"
Foundation: Slab

search online @ eplans.com

**This airy bungalow belongs on the coastline** among palm trees. The smoothly glazed, elongated windows and intricately ornamented openings give the exterior a modern but classy flair. Inside exists a maze of brightly lit, uniquely patterned rooms for entertaining or relaxing. Stunning details include arched and alcove entrances, His and Hers closets, and a wet bar.

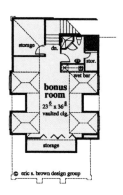

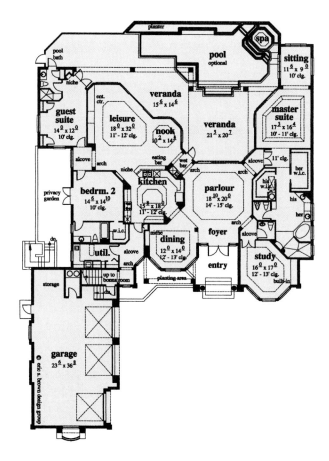

**You'll be amazed at what this estate** has to offer. A study/parlor and a formal dining room announce a grand foyer. Ahead, the living room offers a wet bar and French doors to the rear property. The kitchen is dazzling, with an enormous pantry, oversized cooktop island...even a pizza oven! The gathering room has a corner fireplace and accesses the covered veranda. To the far right, the master suite is a delicious retreat from the world. A bowed window lets in light and a romantic fireplace makes chilly nights cozy. The luxurious bath is awe-inspiring, with a Roman tub and separate compartmented toilet areas—one with a bidet. Upstairs, three family bedrooms share a generous bonus room. A separate pool house is available, which includes a fireplace, full bath, and dressing area.

**plan# HPK1100140**

Style: **FLORIDIAN**
First Floor: 3,307 sq. ft.
Second Floor: 1,642 sq. ft.
Total: 4,949 sq. ft.
Bonus Space: 373 sq. ft.
Bedrooms: 5
Bathrooms: 4½ + ½
Width: 143' - 3"
Depth: 71' - 2"
Foundation: Crawlspace

search online @ eplans.com

REAR EXTERIOR

FIRST FLOOR

SECOND FLOOR

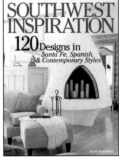

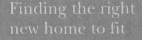

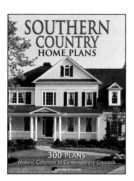

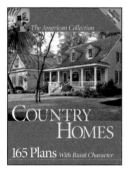
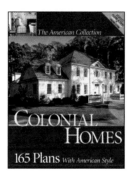
## HANLEY WOOD CONSUMER
One Thomas Circle, NW, Suite 600, Washington, DC 20005

With more than 50 years of experience in the industry and millions of blueprints sold, Hanley Wood is a trusted source of high-quality, high-value pre-drawn home plans.

Using pre-drawn home plans is a **reliable, cost-effective way** to build your dream home, and our vast selection of plans is second-to-none. The nation's finest designers craft these plans that builders know they can trust. Meanwhile, our friendly, knowledgeable customer service representatives can help you every step of the way.

# WHAT YOU'LL GET WITH YOUR ORDER

The contents of each designer's blueprint package is unique, but all contain detailed, high-quality working drawings. You can expect to find the following standard elements in most sets of plans:

## 1. FRONT PERSPECTIVE

This artist's sketch of the exterior of the house gives you an idea of how the house will look when built and landscaped.

## 3. DETAILED FLOOR PLANS

These plans show the layout of each floor of the house. Rooms and interior spaces are carefully dimensioned, doors and windows located, and keys are given for cross-section details provided elsewhere in the plans.

## 2. FOUNDATION AND BASEMENT PLANS

This sheet shows the foundation layout including concrete walls, footings, pads, posts, beams, and bearing walls, and foundation notes. If the home features a basement, the first-floor framing details may also be included on this plan. If your plan features slab construction rather than a basement, the plan shows footings and details for a monolithic slab. This page, or another in the set, may include a sample plot plan for locating your house on a building site. Additional sheets focus on foundation cross-sections and other details.

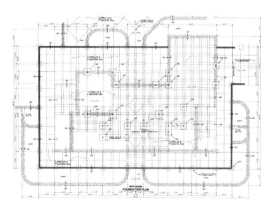

## 4. HOUSE AND DETAIL CROSS-SECTIONS

Large-scale views show sections or cutaways of the foundation, interior walls, exterior walls, floors, stairways, and roof details. Additional cross-sections may show important changes in floor, ceiling, or roof heights, or the relationship of one level to another. These sections show exactly how the various parts of the house fit together and are extremely valuable during construction. Additional sheets may include enlarged wall, floor, and roof construction details.

## 5. ROOF AND FLOOR STRUCTURAL SUPPORTS

The roof and floor framing plans provide detail for these crucial elements of your home. Each includes floor joist, ceiling joist, rafter and roof joist size, spacing, direction, span, and specifications. Beam and window headers, along with necessary details for framing connections, stairways, skylights, or dormers are also included.

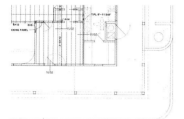

## 6. ELECTRICAL PLAN

The electrical plan offers a detailed outline of all wiring for your home, with notes for all lighting, outlets, switches, and circuits. A layout is provided for each level, as well as basements, garages, or other structures.

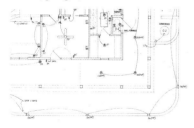

## 7. EXTERIOR ELEVATIONS

In addition to the front exterior, your blueprint set will include drawings of the rear and sides of your house as well. These drawings give notes on exterior materials and finishes. Particular attention is given to cornice detail, brick and stone accents, or other finish items that make your home unique.

# BEFORE YOU CALL

You are making a terrific decision to use a pre-drawn house plan—it is one you can make with confidence, knowing that your blueprints are crafted by national-award-winning certified residential designers and architects, and trusted by builders.

Once you've selected the plan you want—or even if you have questions along the way—our experienced customer service representatives are available 24 hours a day, seven days a week to help you navigate the home-building process. To help them provide you with even better service, please consider the following questions before you call:

**■ Have you chosen or purchased your lot?**
If so, please review the building setback requirements of your local building authority before you call. You don't need to have a lot before ordering plans, but if you own land already, please have the width and depth dimensions handy when you call.

**■ Have you chosen a builder?**
Involving your builder in the plan selection and evaluation process may be beneficial. Luckily, builders know they can have confidence with pre-drawn plans because they've been designed for livability, functionality, and typically are builder-proven at successful home sites across the country.

**■ Do you need a construction loan?**
Construction loans are unique because they involve determining the value of something that is not yet constructed. Several lenders offer convenient contstruction-to-permanent loans. It is important to choose a good lending partner—one who will help guide you through the application and appraisal process. Most will even help you evaluate your contractor to ensure reliability and credit worthiness. Our partnership with IndyMac Bank, a nationwide leader in construction loans, can help you save on your loan, if needed.

**■ How many sets of plans do you need?**
Building a home can typically require a number of sets of blueprints—one for yourself, two or three for the builder and subcontractors, two for the local building department, and one or more for your lender. For this reason, we offer 5- and 8-set plan packages, but your best value is the Reproducible Plan Package. Reproducible plans are accompanied by a license to make modifications and typically up to 12 duplicates of the plan so you have enough copies of the plan for everyone involved in the financing and construction of your home.

**■ Do you want to make any changes to the plan?**
We understand that it is difficult to find blueprints for a home that will meet all of your needs. That is why Hanley Wood is glad to offer plan Customization Services. We will work with you to design the modifications you'd like to see and to adjust your blueprint plans accordingly—anything from changing the foundation; adding square footage, redesigning baths, kitchens, or bedrooms; or most other modifications. This simple, cost-effective service saves you from hiring an outside architect to make alterations. Modifications may only be made to Reproducible Plan Packages that include the license to modify.

**■ Do you have to make any changes to meet local building codes?**
While all of our plans are drawn to meet national building codes at the time they were created, many areas required that plans be stamped by a local engineer to certify that they meet local building codes. Building codes are updated frequently and can vary by state, county, city, or municipality. Contact your local building inspection department, office of planning and zoning, or department of permits to determine how your local codes will affect your construction project. The best way to assure that you can make changes to your plan, if necessary, is to purchase a Reproducible Plan Package.

**■ Has everyone—from family members to contractors—been involved in selecting the plan?**
Building a new home is an exciting process, and using pre-drawn plans is a great way to realize your dreams. Make sure that everyone involved has had an opportunity to review the plan you've selected. While Hanley Wood is the only plans provider with an exchange policy, it's best to be sure all parties agree on your selection before you buy.

## CALL TOLL-FREE 1-800-521-6797

Source Key
HPK11

## CUSTOMIZE YOUR PLAN – HANLEY WOOD CUSTOMIZATION SERVICES

Creating custom home plans has never been easier and more directly accessible. Using state-of-the-art technology and top-performing architectural expertise, Hanley Wood delivers on a long-standing customer commitment to provide world-class home-plans and customization services. Our valued customers—professional home builders and individual home owners—appreciate the convenience and accessibility of this interactive, consultative service.

With the Hanley Wood Customization Service you can:

■ Save valuable time by avoiding drawn-out and frequently repetitive face-to-face design meetings

■ Communicate design and home-plan changes faster and more efficiently
■ Speed-up project turn-around time
■ Build on a budget without sacrificing quality
■ Transform master home plans to suit your design needs and unique personal style

All of our design options and prices are impressively affordable. A detailed quote is available for a $50 consultation fee. Plan modification is an interactive service. Our skilled team of designers will guide you through the customization process from start to finish making recommendations, offering ideas, and determining the feasibility of your changes. This level of service is offered to ensure the final modified plan meets your expectations. If you use our service the $50 fee will be applied to the cost of the modifications.

You may purchase the customization consultation before or after purchasing a plan. In either case, it is necessary to purchase the Reproducible Plan Package and complete the accompanying license to modify the plan before we can begin customization.

**Customization Consultation** . . . . . . . . . . . . . . . . . . . . . . . . . .$50

# TOOLS TO WORK WITH YOUR BUILDER

### Two Reverse Options For Your Convenience – Mirror and Right-Reading Reverse (as available)

Mirror reverse plans simply flip the design 180 degrees—keep in mind, the text will also be flipped. For a minimal fee you can have one or all of your plans shipped mirror reverse, although we recommend having at least one regular set handy. Right-reading reverse plans show the design flipped 180 degrees but the text reads normally. When you choose this option, we ship each set of purchased blueprints in this format.

**Mirror Reverse Fee (indicate the number of sets when ordering)......$55**
**Right Reading Reverse Fee (all sets are reversed)............................$175**

### A Shopping List Exclusively for Your Home – Materials List

A customized Materials List helps you plan and estimate the cost of your new home, outlining the quantity, type, and size of materials needed to build your house (with the exception of mechanical system items). Included are framing lumber, windows and doors, kitchen and bath cabinetry, rough and finished hardware, and much more.

**Materials List** . . . . . . . . . . . . . . . . . . . . . . . . . . . . . . . .$75 each
**Additional Materials Lists (at original time of purchase only)$20 each**

### Plan Your Home-Building Process – Specification Outline

Work with your builder on this step-by-step chronicle of 166 stages or items crucial to the building process. It provides a comprehensive review of the construction process and helps you choose materials.
**Specification Outline** . . . . . . . . . . . . . . . . . . . . . . . . . . .$10 each

### Get Accurate Cost Estimates for Your Home – Quote One® Cost Reports

The Summary Cost Report, the first element in the Quote One® package, breaks down the cost of your home into various categories based on building materials, labor, and installation, and includes three grades of construction: Budget, Standard, and Custom. Make even more informed decisions about your project with the second element of our package, the Material Cost Report. The material and installation cost is shown for each of more than 1,000 line items provided in the standard-grade Materials List, which is included with this tool. Additional space is included for estimates from contractors and subcontractors, such as for mechanical materials, which are not included in our packages.

**Quote One® Summary Cost Report** . . . . . . . . . . . . . . . . . . . . .$35
**Quote One® Detailed Material Cost Report** . . . . . . . . . . . . . .$140*
**\*Detailed material cost report includes the Materials List**

### Learn the Basics of Building – Electrical, Pluming, Mechanical, Construction Detail Sheets

If you want to know more about building techniques—and deal more confidently with your subcontractors—we offer four useful detail sheets. These sheets provide non-plan-specific general information, but are excellent tools that will add to your understanding of Plumbing Details, Electrical Details, Construction Details, and Mechanical Details.

**Electrical Detail Sheet** . . . . . . . . . . . . . . . . . . . . . . . . . . . . .$14.95
**Plumbing Detail Sheet** . . . . . . . . . . . . . . . . . . . . . . . . . . . . .$14.95
**Mechanical Detail Sheet** . . . . . . . . . . . . . . . . . . . . . . . . . . . .$14.95
**Construction Detail Sheet** . . . . . . . . . . . . . . . . . . . . . . . . . . .$14.95

**SUPER VALUE SETS:**
**Buy any 2: $26.95; Buy any 3: $34.95; Buy All 4: $39.95**

**Best Value**

## MAKE YOUR HOME TECH-READY – HOME AUTOMATION UPGRADE

Building a new home provides a unique opportunity to wire it with a plan for future needs. A Home Automation-Ready (HA-Ready) home contains the wiring substructure of tomorrow's connected home. It means that every room—from the front porch to the backyard, and from the attic to the basement—is wired for security, lighting, telecommunications, climate control, home computer networking, whole-house audio, home theater, shade control, video surveillance, entry access control, and yes, video gaming electronic solutions.

Along with the conveniences HA-Ready homes provide, they also have a higher resale value. The Consumer Electronics Association (CEA), in conjunction with the Custom Electronic Design and Installation Association (CEDIA), have developed a TechHome™ Rating system that quantifies the value of HA-Ready homes. The rating system is gaining widespread recognition in the real estate industry.

Developed by CEDIA-certified installers, our Home Automation Upgrade package includes everything you need to work with an installer during the construction of your home. It provides a short explanation of the various subsystems, a wiring floor plan for each level of your home, a detailed materials list with estimated costs, and a list of CEDIA-certified installers in your local area.
**Home Automation Upgrade** . . . . . . . . . . . . . . . .$250

## GET YOUR HOME PLANS PAID FOR!

**IndyMac Bank,** in partnership with Hanley Wood, will reimburse you up to $600 toward the cost of your home plans simply by financing the construction of your new home with IndyMac Bank Home Construction Lending.

IndyMac's construction and permanent loan is a one-time close loan, meaning that one application—and one set of closing fees—provides all the financing you need.

Apply today at www.indymacbank.com, call toll free at 1-866-237-3478, or ask a Hanley Wood customer service representative for details.

## DESIGN YOUR HOME – INTERIOR AND EXTERIOR FINISHING TOUCHES

### Be Your Own Interior Designer! – Home Furniture Planner
Effectively plan the space in your home using our Hands-On Home Furniture Planner. It's fun and easy—no more moving heavy pieces of furniture to see how the room will go together. The kit includes reusable peel-and-stick furniture templates that fit on a 12"x18" laminated layout board—enough space to lay out every room in your house.
**Home Furniture Planning Kit** . . . . . . . . . . . . . . . . . . . . . . . . . . . . . . **$15.95**

### Enjoy the Outdoors! – Deck Plans
Many of our homes have a corresponding deck plan, sold separately, which includes a Deck Plan Frontal Sheet, Deck Framing and Floor Plans, Deck Elevations, and a Deck Materials List. A Standard Deck Details Package, also available, provides all the how-to information necessary for building any deck. Get both the Deck Plan and the Standard Deck Details Package for one low price in our Complete Deck Building Package. See the price tier chart below and call for deck plan availability.
**Deck Details (only)** . . . . . . . . . . . . . . . . . . . . . . . . . . . . . . . . . . . . **$14.95**
**Deck Building Package** . . . . . . . . . . . . . . . . . . . . . . . . . **Plan price + $14.95**

### Create a Professionally Designed Landscape – Landscape Plans
Many of our homes have a front-yard Landscape Plan that is complementary in design to the house plan. These comprehensive Landscape Blueprint Packages include a Frontal Sheet, Plan View, Regionalized Plant & Materials List, a sheet on Planting and Maintaining Your Landscape, Zone Maps, and a Plant Size and Description Guide. Each set of blueprints is a full 18" x 24" with clear, complete instructions in easy-to-read type. Our Landscape Plans are available with a Plant & Materials List adapted by horticultural experts to eight regions of the country. Please specify your region when ordering your plan—see region map below. Call for more information about landscape plan availability and applicable regions.

## LANDSCAPE & DECK PRICE SCHEDULE

| PRICE TIERS | 1-SET STUDY PACKAGE | 5-SET BUILDING PACKAGE | 8-SET BUILDING PACKAGE | 1-SET REPRODUCIBLE* |
|---|---|---|---|---|
| P1 | $25 | $55 | $95 | $145 |
| P2 | $45 | $75 | $115 | $165 |
| P3 | $75 | $105 | $145 | $195 |
| P4 | $105 | $135 | $175 | $225 |
| P5 | $145 | $175 | $215 | $275 |
| P6 | $185 | $215 | $255 | $315 |

PRICES SUBJECT TO CHANGE      * REQUIRES A FAX NUMBER

# TERMS & CONDITIONS

## OUR 90-DAY EXCHANGE POLICY

**BUY WITH CONFIDENCE!**

Hanley Wood is committed to ensuring your satisfaction with your blueprint order, which is why we offer a 90-day exchange policy. With the exception of Reproducible Plan Package orders, we will exchange your entire first order for an equal or greater number of blueprints from our plan collection within 90 days of the original order. The entire content of your original order must be returned before an exchange will be processed. Please call our customer service department at 1-888-690-1116 for your return authorization number and shipping instructions. If the returned blueprints look used, redlined, or copied, we will not honor your exchange. Fees for exchanging your blueprints are as follows: 20% of the amount of the original order, plus the difference in cost if exchanging for a design in a higher price bracket or less the difference in cost if exchanging for a design in a lower price bracket. (Because they can be copied, Reproducible blueprints are not exchangeable or refundable.) Please call for current postage and handling prices. Shipping and handling charges are not refundable.

## ARCHITECTURAL AND ENGINEERING SEALS

Some cities and states now require that a licensed architect or engineer review and "seal" a blueprint, or officially approve it, prior to construction. Prior to application for a building permit or the start of actual construction, we strongly advise that you consult your local building official who can tell you if such a review is required.

## LOCAL BUILDING CODES AND ZONING REQUIREMENTS

Each plan was designed to meet or exceed the requirements of a nationally recognized model building code in effect at the time and place the plan was drawn. Typically plans designed after the year 2000 conform to the International Residential Building Code (IRC 2000 or 2003). The IRC is comprised of portions of the three major codes below. Plans drawn before 2000 conform to one of the three recognized building codes in effect at the time: Building Officials and Code Administrators (BOCA) International, Inc.;

**CALL TOLL-FREE
1-866-473-4052
OR VISIT
EPLANS.COM**

the Southern Building Code Congress International, (SBCCI) Inc.; the International Conference of Building Officials (ICBO); or the Council of American Building Officials (CABO).

Because of the great differences in geography and climate throughout the United States and Canada, each state, county, and municipality has its own building codes, zone requirements, ordinances, and building regulations. Your plan may need to be modified to comply with local requirements. In addition, you may need to obtain permits or inspections from local governments before and in the course of construction. We authorize the use of the blueprints on the express condition that you consult a local licensed architect or engineer of your choice prior to beginning construction and strictly comply with all local building codes, zoning requirements, and other applicable laws, regulations, ordinances, and requirements. Notice: Plans for homes to be built in Nevada must be redrawn by a Nevada-registered professional. Consult your local building official for more information on this subject.

## TERMS AND CONDITIONS

These designs are protected under the terms of United States Copyright Law and may not be copied or reproduced in any way, by

any means, unless you have purchased a Reproducible Plan Package and signed the accompanying license to modify and copy the plan, which clearly indicates your right to modify, copy, or reproduce. We authorize the use of your chosen design as an aid in the construction of ONE (1) single- or multifamily home only. You may not use this design to build a second dwelling or multiple dwellings without purchasing another blueprint or blueprints or paying additional design fees. Multi-use fees vary by designer—please call one of experienced sales representatives for a quote.

## DISCLAIMER

The designers we work with have put substantial care and effort into the creation of their blueprints. However, because we cannot provide on-site consultation, supervision, and control over actual construction, and because of the great variance in local building requirements, building practices, and soil, seismic, weather, and other conditions, WE MAKE NO WARRANTY OF ANY KIND, EXPRESS OR IMPLIED, WITH RESPECT TO THE CONTENT OR USE OF THE BLUEPRINTS, INCLUDING BUT NOT LIMITED TO ANY WARRANTY OF MERCHANTABILITY OR OF FITNESS FOR A PARTICULAR PURPOSE. ITEMS, PRICES, TERMS, AND CONDITIONS ARE SUBJECT TO CHANGE WITHOUT NOTICE.

# IMPORTANT COPYRIGHT NOTICE

*From the Council of Publishing Home Designers*

Blueprints for residential construction (or working drawings, as they are often called in the industry) are copyrighted intellectual property, protected under the terms of the United States Copyright Law and, therefore, cannot be copied legally for use in building. The following are some guidelines to help you get what you need to build your home, without violating copyright law:

## 1. HOME PLANS ARE COPYRIGHTED

Just like books, movies, and songs, home plans receive protection under the federal copyright laws. The copyright laws prevent anyone, other than the copyright owner, from reproducing, modifying, or reusing the plans or design without permission of the copyright owner.

## 2. DO NOT COPY DESIGNS OR FLOOR PLANS FROM ANY PUBLICATION, ELECTRONIC MEDIA, OR EXISTING HOME

It is illegal to copy, change, or redraw home designs found in a plan book, CDROM or on the Internet. The right to modify plans is one of the exclusive rights of copyright. It is also illegal to copy or redraw a constructed home that is protected by copyright, even if you have never seen the plans for the home. If you find a plan or home that you like, you must purchase a set of plans from an authorized source. The plans may not be lent, given away, or sold by the purchaser.

## 3. DO NOT USE PLANS TO BUILD MORE THAN ONE HOUSE

The original purchaser of house plans is typically licensed to build a single home from the plans. Building more than one home from the plans without permission is an infringement of the home designer's copyright. The purchase of a multiple-set package of plans is for the construction of a single home only. The purchase of additional sets of plans does not grant the right to construct more than one home.

## 4. HOUSE PLANS IN THE FORM OF BLUEPRINTS OR BLACKLINES CANNOT BE COPIED OR REPRODUCED

Plans, blueprints, or blacklines, unless they are reproducibles, cannot be copied or reproduced without prior written consent of the copyright owner. Copy shops and blueprinters are prohibited from making copies of these plans without the copyright release letter you receive with reproducible plans.

## 5. HOUSE PLANS IN THE FORM OF BLUEPRINTS OR BLACKLINES CANNOT BE REDRAWN

Plans cannot be modified or redrawn without first obtaining the copyright owner's permission. With your purchase of plans, you are licensed to make non-structural changes by "red-lining" the purchased plans. If you need to make structural changes or need to redraw the plans for any reason, you must purchase a reproducible set of plans (see topic 6) which includes a license to modify the plans. Blueprints do not come with a license to make structural changes or to redraw the plans. You may not reuse or sell the modified design.

## 6. REPRODUCIBILE HOME PLANS

Reproducible plans (for example sepias, mylars, CAD files, electronic files, and vellums) come with a license to make modifications to the plans. Once modified, the plans can be taken to a local copy shop or blueprinter to make up to 10 or 12 copies of the plans to use in the construction of a single home. Only one home can be constructed from any single purchased set of reproducible plans either in original form or as modified. The license to modify and copy must be completed and returned before the plan will be shipped.

## 7. MODIFIED DESIGNS CANNOT BE REUSED

Even if you are licensed to make modifications to a copyrighted design, the modified design is not free from the original designer's copyright. The sale or reuse of the modified design is prohibited. Also, be aware that any modification to plans relieves the original designer from liability for design defects and voids all warranties expressed or implied.

## 8. WHO IS RESPONSIBLE FOR COPYRIGHT INFRINGEMENT?

Any party who participates in a copyright violation may be responsible including the purchaser, designers, architects, engineers, drafters, homeowners, builders, contractors, sub-contractors, copy shops, blueprinters, developers, and real estate agencies. It does not matter whether or not the individual knows that a violation is being committed. Ignorance of the law is not a valid defense.

## 9. PLEASE RESPECT HOME DESIGN COPYRIGHTS

In the event of any suspected violation of a copyright, or if there is any uncertainty about the plans purchased, the publisher, architect, designer, or the Council of Publishing Home Designers (www.cphd.org) should be contacted before proceeding. Awards are sometimes offered for information about home design copyright infringement.

## 10. PENALTIES FOR INFRINGEMENT

Penalties for violating a copyright may be severe. The responsible parties are required to pay actual damages caused by the infringement (which may be substantial), plus any profits made by the infringer commissions to include all profits from the sale of any home built from an infringing design. The copyright law also allows for the recovery of statutory damages, which may be as high as $150,000 for each infringement. Finally, the infringer may be required to pay legal fees which often exceed the damages.

## BLUEPRINT PRICE SCHEDULE

| PRICE TIERS | 1-SET STUDY PACKAGE | 5-SET BUILDING PACKAGE | 8-SET BUILDING PACKAGE | 1-SET REPRODUCIBLE* |
|---|---|---|---|---|
| A1 | $450 | $500 | $555 | $675 |
| A2 | $490 | $545 | $595 | $735 |
| A3 | $540 | $605 | $665 | $820 |
| A4 | $590 | $660 | $725 | $895 |
| C1 | $640 | $715 | $775 | $950 |
| C2 | $690 | $760 | $820 | $1025 |
| C3 | $735 | $810 | $875 | $1100 |
| C4 | $785 | $860 | $925 | $1175 |
| L1 | $895 | $990 | $1075 | $1335 |
| L2 | $970 | $1065 | $1150 | $1455 |
| L3 | $1075 | $1175 | $1270 | $1600 |
| L4 | $1185 | $1295 | $1385 | $1775 |
| SQ1 | | | | .40/SQ. FT. |
| SQ3 | | | | .55/SQ. FT. |
| SQ5 | | | | .80/SQ. FT. |

PRICES SUBJECT TO CHANGE

* REQUIRES A FAX NUMBER

| PLAN # | PRICE TIER | PAGE | MATERIALS LIST | QUOTE ONE® | DECK | DECK PRICE | LANDSCAPE | LANDSCAPE PRICE | REGIONS |
|---|---|---|---|---|---|---|---|---|---|
| HPK1100001 | SQ1 | 22 | Y | | | | | | |
| HPK1100002 | C4 | 26 | | | | | | | |
| HPK1100003 | SQ1 | 30 | | | | | | | |
| HPK1100004 | SQ1 | 34 | | | | | | | |
| HPK1100005 | L2 | 35 | | | | | | | |
| HPK1100006 | L1 | 36 | | | | | | | |
| HPK1100007 | SQ1 | 37 | Y | Y | | | | | |
| HPK1100008 | C4 | 38 | | | | | | | |
| HPK1100009 | C3 | 39 | | | | | | | |
| HPK1100010 | C4 | 40 | | | | | | | |
| HPK1100011 | C2 | 41 | | | | | | | |
| HPK1100012 | C3 | 42 | | | | | | | |
| HPK1100013 | C2 | 43 | | | | | | | |
| HPK1100014 | C4 | 44 | | | | | | | |
| HPK1100015 | C3 | 45 | | | | | | | |
| HPK1100016 | C2 | 46 | | | | | | | |
| HPK1100017 | C2 | 47 | | | | | | | |
| HPK1100018 | A4 | 48 | | | | | | | |
| HPK1100019 | C3 | 49 | | | | | | | |
| HPK1100020 | A4 | 50 | | | | | | | |
| HPK1100021 | L2 | 51 | | | | | | | |
| HPK1100022 | C3 | 52 | | | | | | | |
| HPK1100023 | C2 | 53 | Y | | | | | | |
| HPK1100024 | A4 | 54 | Y | Y | ODA012 | P3 | OLA083 | P3 | 12345678 |
| HPK1100025 | C1 | 55 | Y | | ODA012 | P3 | OLA010 | P3 | 1234568 |

| PLAN # | PRICE TIER | PAGE | MATERIALS LIST | QUOTE ONE® | DECK | DECK PRICE | LANDSCAPE | LANDSCAPE PRICE | REGIONS |
|---|---|---|---|---|---|---|---|---|---|
| HPK1100026 | C3 | 56 | Y | | | | | | |
| HPK1100027 | C3 | 57 | Y | | | | | | |
| HPK1100028 | SQ1 | 58 | | | | | | | |
| HPK1100029 | C1 | 59 | Y | | | | | | |
| HPK1100030 | C2 | 60 | Y | | | | | | |
| HPK1100031 | C2 | 61 | | | | | | | |
| HPK1100032 | A4 | 62 | | | | | | | |
| HPK1100033 | SQ3 | 63 | | | | | | | |
| HPK1100034 | SQ3 | 64 | | | | | | | |
| HPK1100035 | C2 | 65 | Y | | | | | | |
| HPK1100036 | SQ1 | 66 | Y | | | | | | |
| HPK1100037 | SQ1 | 67 | Y | | ODA011 | P2 | OLA088 | P4 | 12345678 |
| HPK1100038 | A4 | 68 | Y | | | | | | |
| HPK1100039 | C1 | 69 | Y | | | | | | |
| HPK1100040 | C1 | 70 | Y | | | | | | |
| HPK1100041 | C1 | 71 | Y | | | | | | |
| HPK1100042 | L1 | 72 | | | | | | | |
| HPK1100043 | L2 | 73 | | | | | | | |
| HPK1100044 | C3 | 74 | | | | | | | |
| HPK1100045 | C2 | 75 | | | | | | | |
| HPK1100046 | C2 | 76 | Y | Y | | | OLA007 | P4 | 1234568 |
| HPK1100047 | A3 | 77 | | | | | | | |
| HPK1100048 | L1 | 79 | Y | Y | ODA008 | P3 | OLA016 | P4 | 1234568 |
| HPK1100049 | SQ1 | 82 | | | | | | | |
| HPK1100050 | C1 | 83 | Y | | ODA015 | P2 | OLA007 | P4 | 1234568 |

| PLAN # | PRICE TIER | PAGE | MATERIALS LIST | QUOTE ONE® | DECK | DECK PRICE | LANDSCAPE | LANDSCAPE PRICE | REGIONS |
|---|---|---|---|---|---|---|---|---|---|
| HPK1100051 | C4 | 84 | | | | | | | |
| HPK1100052 | C4 | 85 | | | | | | | |
| HPK1100053 | L1 | 86 | Y | Y | ODA002 | P2 | OLA015 | P4 | 123568 |
| HPK1100054 | C4 | 87 | | | | | | | |
| HPK1100055 | L2 | 88 | | | | | | | |
| HPK1100056 | L2 | 89 | | | | | | | |
| HPK1100057 | C3 | 90 | | | | | | | |
| HPK1100058 | SQ1 | 91 | | | | | | | |
| HPK1100059 | C3 | 92 | | | | | | | |
| HPK1100060 | L1 | 93 | Y | | | | | | |
| HPK1100061 | L1 | 94 | | | | | | | |
| HPK1100062 | SQ1 | 95 | Y | Y | | | | | |
| HPK1100063 | L1 | 96 | | | | | | | |
| HPK1100064 | C4 | 97 | | | | | | | |
| HPK1100065 | C1 | 98 | | | | | | | |
| HPK1100066 | C3 | 99 | | | | | | | |
| HPK1100067 | L1 | 100 | | | | | | | |
| HPK1100068 | C2 | 101 | | | | | | | |
| HPK1100069 | C4 | 102 | | | | | | | |
| HPK1100070 | C4 | 103 | | | | | | | |
| HPK1100071 | C2 | 104 | | | | | | | |
| HPK1100072 | L2 | 105 | | | | | | | |
| HPK1100073 | C3 | 106 | | | | | | | |
| HPK1100074 | C2 | 107 | Y | Y | ODA012 | P3 | OLA003 | P3 | 123568 |
| HPK1100075 | L1 | 108 | | | | | | | |
| HPK1100076 | C4 | 109 | Y | | | | | | |
| HPK1100077 | C2 | 110 | | | | | | | |
| HPK1100078 | SQ1 | 111 | Y | Y | | | | | |
| HPK1100079 | C3 | 112 | | | | | | | |
| HPK1100080 | SQ3 | 114 | | | | | | | |
| HPK1100081 | SQ1 | 118 | | | | | | | |
| HPK1100082 | SQ1 | 119 | | | | | | | |
| HPK1100083 | L3 | 120 | | | | | | | |
| HPK1100084 | L1 | 121 | | | | | | | |
| HPK1100085 | L1 | 122 | | | | | | | |
| HPK1100086 | C2 | 123 | | | | | | | |
| HPK1100087 | C4 | 124 | | | | | | | |
| HPK1100088 | L1 | 125 | | | | | | | |
| HPK1100089 | C2 | 126 | | | | | | | |
| HPK1100090 | C1 | 127 | | | | | | | |
| HPK1100091 | C3 | 128 | | | | | | | |
| HPK1100092 | C2 | 129 | | | | | | | |
| HPK1100093 | C2 | 130 | | | | | | | |
| HPK1100094 | C2 | 131 | | | | | | | |
| HPK1100095 | C2 | 132 | | | | | | | |
| HPK1100096 | C3 | 133 | | | | | | | |
| HPK1100097 | C3 | 134 | | | | | | | |
| HPK1100098 | L1 | 135 | | | | | | | |
| HPK1100099 | L1 | 136 | | | | | | | |
| HPK1100100 | SQ1 | 137 | | | | | | | |
| HPK1100101 | C2 | 138 | | | | | | | |
| HPK1100102 | C4 | 139 | | | | | | | |
| HPK1100103 | A4 | 140 | | | | | | | |
| HPK1100104 | A3 | 141 | | | | | | | |
| HPK1100105 | C3 | 142 | | | | | | | |
| HPK1100106 | SQ3 | 144 | Y | | | | | | |
| HPK1100107 | SQ1 | 148 | | | | | | | |
| HPK1100108 | SQ1 | 149 | Y | | | | OLA008 | P4 | 1234568 |
| HPK1100109 | C3 | 150 | Y | | | | | | |
| HPK1100110 | C1 | 151 | | | | | | | |
| HPK1100111 | C1 | 152 | | | | | | | |
| HPK1100112 | C2 | 153 | | | | | | | |
| HPK1100113 | A4 | 154 | | | | | | | |
| HPK1100114 | C3 | 155 | | | | | OLA012 | P3 | 12345678 |
| HPK1100115 | C1 | 156 | | | | | | | |
| HPK1100116 | C3 | 157 | Y | | | | OLA004 | P3 | 123568 |
| HPK1100117 | SQ3 | 158 | | | | | | | |
| HPK1100118 | SQ1 | 159 | Y | | | | | | |
| HPK1100119 | C1 | 160 | | | | | | | |
| HPK1100120 | SQ1 | 161 | | | | | | | |
| HPK1100121 | C1 | 162 | Y | | | | | | |
| HPK1100122 | SQ1 | 163 | | | | | | | |
| HPK1100123 | C2 | 164 | Y | | | | | | |
| HPK1100124 | C3 | 165 | | | | | OLA004 | P3 | 123568 |
| HPK1100125 | SQ1 | 166 | | | | | | | |
| HPK1100126 | L1 | 167 | | | | | | | |
| HPK1100127 | L2 | 168 | Y | Y | | | OLA024 | P4 | 123568 |
| HPK1100128 | SQ1 | 169 | Y | Y | | | OLA001 | P3 | 123568 |
| HPK1100129 | C1 | 170 | Y | | | | | | |
| HPK1100130 | A4 | 171 | Y | | | | | | |
| HPK1100131 | C3 | 172 | | | | | | | |
| HPK1100132 | SQ1 | 173 | | | | | | | |
| HPK1100133 | C1 | 174 | | | | | | | |
| HPK1100134 | SQ3 | 175 | | | | | | | |
| HPK1100135 | C1 | 176 | | | | | | | |
| HPK1100136 | A4 | 177 | | | | | | | |
| HPK1100137 | C1 | 178 | | | | | | | |
| HPK1100138 | C1 | 179 | | | | | | | |
| HPK1100139 | SQ1 | 180 | | | | | | | |
| HPK1100140 | SQ1 | 181 | Y | | | | | | |

# Final Detail

Traditional-style furniture complements this new Southern dining room, with its deep windows, lavish crown molding, and gracefully ornamented ceiling. It is clearly a gathering spot for future generations. For more on this home, see page 82.